Seven Months in the Rebel States During the North American War, 1863

Captain J. Scheibert.

Seeing the Elephant: Southern Eyewitnesses to the Civil War
Series Editors
Gary W. Gallagher • Robert K. Krick

Seven Months in the Rebel States During the North American War, 1863

CAPTAIN JUSTUS SCHEIBERT

Translated from the German by
JOSEPH C. HAYES

Edited with an Introduction by
W. STANLEY HOOLE

2009 Introduction by
ROBERT K. KRICK

The University of Alabama Press
Tuscaloosa

The University of Alabama Press
Tuscaloosa, Alabama 35487-0380

∞

The paper on which this book is printed meets the minimum requirements
of American National Standard for Information Sciences-Permanence of
Paper for Printed Library Materials, ANSI Z39.48-1984.

Library of Congress Cataloging-in-Publication Data

Library of Congress Cataloging-in-Publication Data

Scheibert, J. (Justus), 1831–1903.
  [Sieben monate in den rebellen-staaten während des nordamerikanisch-
en krieges 1863. English]
  Seven months in the rebel states during the North American war, 1863 /
Justus Scheibert ; translated from the German by Joseph C. Hayes ; edited
with an introduction by W.M. Stanley Hoole.
     p. cm. — (Seeing the elephant—Southern eyewitnesses to the Civil
War)
  Originally published as: Sieben monate in den rebellen-staaten während
des nordamerikanischen krieges 1863. Stetttin : T. von der Nahmer, 1868.
Previously published in English: Tuscaloosa, Ala. : Confederate Pub. Co.,
1958.
  Includes bibliographical references and index.
  ISBN 978-0-8173-5591-3 (pbk. : alk. paper) —
  ISBN 978-0-8173-8294-0 (electronic) 1. United States—History—Civil
War, 1861-1865—Campaigns. I. Hoole, William Stanley, 1903– II. Title.
  E470.S323 2009
  973.7'3—dc22

                                                         2009015505

Series Editor Introduction

For Justus Scheibert, *Seven Months in the Rebel States During the North American War, 1863*

Justus Scheibert's *Seven Months in the Rebel States* serves as a splendid inaugural volume for "Seeing the Elephant: Southern Eyewitnesses to the Civil War." Though not southern by birth or residence, Scheibert certainly should be reckoned a Confederate by association. He traveled through the Carolinas and Virginia, accompanied Robert E. Lee's Army of Northern Virginia during the famous campaigns of Chancellorsville and Gettysburg, and thoroughly identified with the civilians and soldiers who acted as his hosts. A captain in the Prussian army, Scheibert focused his critical eye on military events and topics, while also commenting about political, economic, and social dimensions of the Confederacy. Many descriptive passages create memorable images of the Confederate countryside and of cities such as Richmond and Charleston. Scheibert's observations convey a strong impression of a Rebel *nation*—with its government, armies, and people struggling to establish themselves among the national entities of the western world.

Scheibert's perceptive narrative of Lee's spring and summer campaigning in 1863 will likely prove most appealing to readers. As Robert K. Krick's introduction makes clear, *Seven Months in the Rebel States* abounds with perceptive biographical detail about Lee and a number of his subordinates (as well as about Jefferson Davis). In this regard, Capt. Scheibert belongs alongside Lt. Col. Arthur James Lyon Fremantle, the famous British observer, as a chronicler of the Army of Northern Virginia and its high command. Enhanced by Krick's introduction and for the first time indexed properly, this edition of an underappreciated classic should win many new admirers among both scholars and lay readers.

Gary W. Gallagher

Contents

Illustrations

2009 Introduction by Robert K. Krick

As General R. E. Lee watched his troops complete the victory at Chancellorsville on May 3, 1863, he commented about those stalwart soldiers to Prussian observer Justus Scheibert. With "Stonewall" Jackson recently wounded—mortally as events would prove—Lee had been obliged to throw himself directly into managing operations. Scheibert rode up next to the renowned general near Hazel Grove, the key terrain feature on the battlefield, as Southern infantry swarmed across the intervening ridge toward the Chancellorsville intersection.

"No more frightful place can be imagined," Scheibert wrote in recalling the terror and drama. Lee's conversation turned to the men who were fighting under his direction. In the midst of the flying bullets, the general talked of educating them for postwar life: "The state is to be made up of them in the future—they are later to pursue peaceful occupations and to practice quiet civic virtues. . . . One must accustom the men as well as possible to self-control."

Frank's encounters of that sort, of an intimate tone and at the highest levels of the Army of Northern Virginia, make Justus Scheibert's narrative a major source on Lee and his army.

The same propinquity that afforded Scheibert a priceless observation point also left him a prejudiced witness. He admired the Confederacy's famous Virginian leaders, and grew deeply fond of several staff officers. The memoir readily slips into first-person pronouns when referring to Confederate matters—Southerners become "we" and "us." Readers will quickly recognize the enthusiastic endorsements, and must factor in the parochial viewpoint.

Despite an obvious partisanship, Scheibert remained willing to criticize his hosts and friends. He suspected Lee of "excessive caution" after the battle of Fredericksburg, noted faulty Southern attitudes toward ordnance improvements, and condemned lackadaisical approaches to drill and camp regimen and discipline in general.

Two brief and easily overlooked references in *Seven Months in the Rebel States* carry immense weight in evaluating the memoir's credibility, by establishing that the author kept a diary documenting his experiences. Amid the helter-skelter Confederate reaction to surprise at Brandy Station, Scheibert thought with chagrin of the apparent loss of his journal when Federal horseman overran Stuart's headquarters. To his delight, the cavalry's diligent chief quartermaster, Major Norman R. Fitzhugh, had managed to hustle everyone's belongings to safety, including the invaluable diary.

The importance of having the diary as a contemporary record, when Scheibert began to write his narrative a few years later, can be seen in a steady succession of reliable anecdotes. Most memoirs, even without the language complication affecting the Prussian visitor, garble the names of principles. Fleeting encounters almost never yield verifiable names or facts.

By contrast, every episode in *Seven Months in the Rebel States* that can be thoroughly checked stands up to examination. For example, as he rode south up the Shenandoah Valley late in July 1863, Scheibert encountered a friendly civilian who became a congenial traveling companion. The "Rev. Dr. Deems from Wilson, North Carolina" had gone to Lee's army in search of "his mortally wounded and captured son." The facts match without a single anomaly. Lieutenant Theodore DeSaussure Deems of the 5th North Carolina, age 19—one of a dreadfully long casualty list butchered through General Alfred Iverson's incompetence—died in Federal hands in the aftermath of Gettysburg. His father, the 1860 census reveals, was the Rev. Charles F. Deems of Wilson.

The encounter with Deems is not, of course, of surpassing significance, despite its evocative human-interest texture. As exemplar of Scheibert's accuracy, however, the story and others like it establish strong credibility. That validation buttresses the worth of the Prussian observer's reports on matters of more consequence.

Scheibert wrote *Sieben Monate* just four years after most of the events he witnessed. That timely proximity, combined with the diary as guide, puts his narrative far ahead of the vast majority of primary accounts of Chancellorsville and Gettysburg. The unusual perspective afforded by his foreign origins, added to the early date of the memoir and the salutary impact of the diary, produced an account of notable import. Scheibert's ebullient personality and inquisitive nature made him an ideal observer-narrator.

This new release of *Seven Months in the Rebel States During the North American War, 1863* is taken directly and without change from the book's first appearance in an English translation, in 1958. That edition, edited by William Stanley Hoole (1903–1990) of the University of Alabama, was part of an extensive series, the "Confederate Centennial Studies." Hoole's introduction appears intact here. It supplies Scheibert's biographical background.

The few editing errors in the 1958 edition survive in the body of this version, but are corrected in the index. On page 87, for instance, Scheibert mentions "General Jones" as the cavalry commander rallying his troops just north of Stuart's headquarters on June 9, 1863, at Brandy Station. The 1958 editing supplies the general's name as John M. Jones, a newly promoted infantry brigadier who in fact was many miles distant. The Brandy Station officer, General William Edmondson Jones (who wore the well-earned *nom de guerre* of "Grumble"), appears accurately in the index.

The entirely new index in this 2009 edition also pries open the gist of Scheibert's book by affording access to a wide array of important topics. The 1958 index tracked only people and places, without breaking down even those entries. That missed much of the memoir's most valuable content, which deals with subjective topics: tactics and strategy, especially involving cavalry; plundering; European attitudes toward the war; how couriers and scouts functioned; fortifications—Scheibert's special focus, as assigned; ordnance, including resistance to rifled weapons; attitudes toward blacks; engineering; and many more.

The 1958 edition elicited strong plaudits for its obvious merits. In a survey of thirty books in *The Journal of Southern History*, Wendell Holmes Stephenson applauded Scheibert's "vivid impressions, observations, and characterizations." In *The Mississippi Valley Historical Review*, Grady McWhiney called the memoir "valuable" and, despite the unmistakable Southern sympathies, "not completely partisan." In a short, crisply insightful analysis, McWhiney captured Scheibert's greatest strength: "he described the organization, weapons, dress, habits, camp routine, and tactics of Lee's army better than any other foreign observer."

Civil War Books, A Critical Bibliography, a 1967 publication by Louisiana State University Press, provides only a line or two of comment on each title by editors Allan Nevins, Bell I. Wiley, and James I. Robertson, Jr. They found the 1868 Stettin version "sometimes revealing." The editing of the 1958 translation into English, they grumbled tersely, "is not as full as one would have desired." Exhaustive editing always deserves applause; but the mere delivery of Scheibert into a format accessible to American readers surely was achievement enough to earn Hoole strong plaudits.

Hoole's "Confederate Centennial Studies" eventually reached twenty-six volumes in addition to *Seven Months in the Rebel States*. He produced only 450 copies of each title, and sold them for $4 each by subscription. Two other books in the set fit snugly next to Scheibert's memoir: volumes by and about his fellow European observers, Frank Vizetelly and Francis C. Lawley. Several other titles proved their importance, such as the only major set of published letters by a member of the Confederate States Marine Corps.

Thomas W. Broadfoot of Wilmington, North Carolina, republished the entire Centennial Series in 2001, including an additional twenty-eighth volume about Hoole and the set.

Anyone interested in Justus Scheibert should be aware of three other invaluable publications that expand his story and illuminate his life. The best analysis of his military writing remains an article more than a half-century old. "A Prussian Observer with Lee," by the late Jay Luvaas (1927–2009), in the Autumn 1957 issue of *Military Affairs* (Vol. 21, No. 3) evaluates Scheibert's writings with admirable perspective and detail. The first-rate article justifies Luvaas's reputation as a leading student of foreign observers and American military matters.

Two books published since the 1958 edition finally make available in English most of Scheibert's other writings on the American Civil War. A German firm had published his collaboration with Heros von Borcke on the battle of Brandy Station, its Vorwort signed jointly in type in Berlin in August 1893. *Die grosse Reiterschlacht bei Brandy Station, 9. Juni 1863* ran to 179 pages, plus a page advertising a new edition of von Borcke's *Mit Prinz Friedrich Karl*. Five good maps and several striking illustrations (most drawn by Scheibert himself, quite significantly) illuminated the text. In his *The South to Posterity*, Douglas Southall Freeman touted the book's "elaborate maps" and "careful tactical explanations," and concluded that the Scheibert and von Borcke volume "is today the best account of the greatest cavalry battle ever fought in the Western world." That judgment remains valid, although serious research now afoot may finally yield a definitive modern study of Brandy Station.

In November 1976, Palaemon Press of Winston-Salem, North Carolina, published an excellent translation, *The Great Cavalry Battle of Brandy Station*. It included a forward by Bell I. Wiley and a new introduction by the translator-editors. All 1,000 copies had paper wraps, but fine production values. The publisher asked $10 for the book. Early in 2009, the major Internet used-book sources offered the 1976 edition for $75, and the 1893 for $700 or more.

The recent translation, by Professor Frederic Trautmann of Temple University, of two other books comes close to completing an English-language Scheibert Civil War canon. *A Prussian Observes the American Civil War: The Military Studies of Justus Scheibert* (University of Missouri Press, 2001) prints thoughtful treatises that had theretofore existed only in original German or other European editions: *Der Burgerkrieg in den Nordamerikanishcen Staaten: Militarisch beleuchetet fur den deutschen Offizier* (Berlin, 1874) and *Das Zusammenwirken der Armee und Marine. Eine Studie illustriert durch den Kampf um den Mississippi, 1861–1863* (Rathenow, 1887?). For some reason, Trautmann gerrymandered the content of the two volumes into a single text, leaving their original formats indistinguishable. He also did not supply annotations of much scope.

Though important, the Trautmann translations will not fully enrapture a casual student of the war, although some early pages in "The Civil War in the North American States" include priceless vignettes of Lee, Jackson, and Stuart. Physical descriptions of each famous officer also discuss style and substance. Lee, Scheibert concluded, "could be summed up in a word, *calm*" [his emphasis]. He describes Jackson's loss to Lee, in quintessentially Teutonic terms, as "a Blucher who lost his Gneisenau." And Stuart, not surprisingly, seemed to him "the model of the dashing cavalry leader."

The Prussian's ardor for mounted operations shows through in these studies. His chapter on cavalry operations and lessons learned stretches longer than the similar segments on infantry and artillery combined. His own lofty principles resonate in such subjects as "What Morality Meant to the Armed Forces," in which Scheibert suggests Europeans should "learn from the American war . . .

the value of rectitude." That high-minded notion, of course, both misrepresented the American war to a considerable degree and fell on starkly fallow European ground.

Scheibert's examination of "Cooperation of the Army and Navy" deserves attention as a groundbreaking study of the vital question of joint military endeavors. Standard studies of the war paid but little attention to combined operations, and down to the modern era the topic has been given remarkably short shrift. Trautmann declares it to be "the first study of combined operations anywhere ever."

The extensive body of military writings that poured from Scheibert's pen across nearly four decades consisted primarily of serious analyses, but he aimed a few at a more popular readership. His work on the Franco-Prussian War would be considered a coffee-table book in modern parlance. *Der Krieg zwischen Deutschland und Frankreich in den Jahren 1870/71* (Leipzig, 1889) covers that entire complex conflict. It features a brightly colorful heroic decoration on the front board and includes dozens of dramatic illustrations, many in full-page format.

A book that appeared just a few months before he died reveals Scheibert still enamored of lost causes, and again writing for popular consumption. *Der Freiheitskampf der Buren und de Geschichte ihres Landes* (Berlin, 1903) also displays a spectacularly heroic color decoration on the front board, and an array of dramatically popularized illustrations. The "Freedom Struggle" of the Boers obviously appealed to the author's romantic nature, probably with some nostalgic parallels to his youthful American adventures.

Nothing that Justus Scheibert wrote, whether analytical or popular, resonates with the personal investment that shows through the narrative in *Seven Months in the Rebel States*. His frank admission (page 35) of the emotional impact of his experiences reveals what gives the book its special cachet. In his weeks at the headquarters of the Army of Northern Virginia, Scheibert declared, "I was . . . to enjoy the most stirring, and thus the finest days of my life." His description of those days, informed by a contemporary diary and invigorated by his zest and verve, makes for a really splendid book.

Robert K. Krick
Fredericksburg, Virginia

Introduction

MANY OF THE BOOKS written by foreigners who cast their lots with the Confederate States of America are well known and widely quoted,[1] but a few, especially those in non-English languages, have received comparatively scant recognition. For instance, Charles Frédéric Girard's *Les États Confédérés d'Amerique Visités en 1863* (Paris, 1864), recounting his experiences with both the military and civilian Confederacy, has not been translated.[2] Neither has *Die grosse Reiterschlacht bei Brandy Station . . .* (Berlin, 1893), written by Heros von Borcke and Justus Scheibert, Prussian compatriots, despite the fact that Douglas Southall Freeman described it as "the fullest study of the action of June 9, 1863."[3] But in several respects the most neglected writing is perhaps that of Captain Justus Scheibert, "Jeb" Stuart's "fighting observer," whose three books (in addition to the collaboration mentioned above) have received precious little attention from historians. His *Das Zusammenwirken der Armee und Marine . . . 1861-63* (Rathenow, [1887]), for instance, a careful analysis of naval affairs along the Mississippi, has not been put into English. His *Der Bürgerkrieg in den nordamerikanischen Staaten . . .* (Berlin, 1874), a splendid account of Confederate infantry, cavalry, artillery, and engineer strategy, was promptly translated into French as *La Guerre Civile aux États-Unis d'Amerique . . .* (Paris, 1876), but the volume has not yet been made available to English readers. Freeman has described this study as "especially important for its statement of Lee's

---

[1] See Ella Lonn, *Foreigners in the Confederacy* (Chapel Hill, 1940).
[2] An English translation of Girard's book is now being prepared for publication as a number in the Confederate Centennial Studies.
[3] *R. E. Lee: A Biography* (New York, 1935), IV, 557.

theory of the function of the high command."[4]   And Scheibert's *Sieben Monate in den Rebellen-Staaten während des
nordamerikanischen Krieges 1863* (Stettin, 1868), containing vivid portrayals of the battles of Chancellorsville,
Brandy Station, and Gettysburg, records of personal conversations with President Jefferson Davis, Generals Lee,
Jackson, Beauregard, and Stuart and many observations on
life in the Confederacy, has up to now been available in the
original German only—yet, nearly seventy years ago Charles
Poindexter, distinguished historian and librarian, pronounced it a study "marked with good sense and power of
observation," one that "well deserves translation as a
valuable contribution to the history of the time."[5]

Captain Justus Scheibert, a prolific writer of military
treatises, was born on May 16, 1831 in Stettin, Pomerania
(now Szczecin, Poland), the oldest of eleven children.   In
1849 he joined the Prussian Army.   A year later he passed
officer examinations and for a decade thereafter served at
Glogau, Magdeburg, Silberberg, Neisse and other military
posts.   In January, 1863, as Captain Scheibert, he was
ordered by Prince von Radziwill, chief of the Prussian
Engineer Corps, to proceed at once to the "North American
war threatre" as an observer.   Already well known as an
authority on fortifications, he was instructed especially to
study "the effect of rifled cannon fire on earth, masonry,
and iron, and the operation of armor on land and at sea."[6]

---

[4] *Ibid.*, IV, 560.   Freeman must have erred when he stated that
Der Bürgerkrieg . . . has been translated into English.   In Scheibert's
autobiography, *Mit Schwert und Feder. Erinnerungen aus meinem
Leben* (Berlin, 1902), p. 343, it is suggested that the work had been
or would be Englished, but no title, date, or place of publication is
given.   During a two-year period this writer has diligently searched
the libraries of the United States and Europe for an English version
and has in every instance met with negative results.   The same experience has befallen Jay Luvaas ("A Prussian Observer with Lee,"
Military Affairs, XXI, 107, Fall, 1957).   Perhaps, Freeman was mis-
led by a letter Scheibert wrote to the *Southern Historical Society
Papers* (see Col. C. S. Venable, "Major Scheibert's Book," IV, 90,
Aug., 1877).   This journal is hereinafter cited as *SHSP*.
[5] "Major J. Scheibert (of the Prussian Army) on Confederate
History," *ibid.*, XVIII, 422 (Dec., 1890).
[6] *Mit Schwert und Feder*, pp. 4, 607, 11-33, 111; *Die grosse Reiter-*

Originally, Radziwill had planned to send Scheibert to the United States Army, but the Captain, a strong Southern sympathizer, believed that his mission could best be accomplished by attaching himself to the Confederacy—and the Prussian high command agreed.[7]

Armed with letters of introduction from Confederate Agent James M. Mason to Secretary of War James A. Seddon, Captain Scheibert arrived in Charleston on March 15. He was warmly received by General P. G. T. Beauregard. Two weeks later, he went on to the headquarters of the Army of Northern Virginia beside the Rappahannock, where General Robert E. Lee extended him every courtesy.

Scheibert remained at Lee's headquarters ten days, until April 19, during which time he became well acquainted with Generals "Jeb" Stuart and "Stonewall" Jackson and Major Charles S. Venable, one of Lee's aides, visited the battlefield at Fredericksburg, observed Confederate infantry, artillery, and cavalry drills, and otherwise shared the austere yet oft-times pleasant camp life of his high-ranking hosts. Meantime, much to his delight, he met a distinguished fellow-countryman, Colonel Heros von Borcke, also of the Prussian Engineer Corps, who had been with Stuart for a year and was serving as his chief-of-staff. Upon Stuart's and Borcke's urgent requests, Scheibert decided to visit Stuart's headquarters near Culpeper which, after a short trip to Richmond, he reached on April 21.

As a member of Stuart's staff, Scheibert served as *Rittmeister*—that is, as sort of handyman, making maps, helping on bridge and breastwork constructions, carrying messages and otherwise making himself useful. And during

---

schlacht . . . , p. 178; and Justus Scheibert, *Einfluss der neuesten Taktik und der gezogenen Waffen auf den Festungskrieg* . . . (Berlin, 1861).

[7] Wilhelm Kaufmann, *Die Deutschen im amerikanischen Bürgerkriege (Sezessionskrieg 1861-1865)* (München und Berlin, 1911), p. 366; *Mit Schwert und Feder*, p. 135; *Die grosse Reiterschlacht* . . . , pp. 178-179. Most Prussian officers who came to America sympathized with the South. Scheibert had doubtless planned from the beginning not to "observe" in the North, "but for diplomatic reasons, since the Confederacy was not recognized by the European powers, the Prussian government chose not to order him south" (Luvaas, XXI, 106, Fall, 1957). See Lonn, pp. 223ff.

the weeks that followed he endeared himself to all who knew him—especially the ladies in nearby Culpeper. As Borcke wrote later, Scheibert delighted them with "his excellent piano-forte playing, to say nothing of the amusement they derived from his original practice with the idiom and pronunciation of the English language."[8]   According to Lieutenant-Colonel William W. Blackford, Stuart's adjutant, Scheibert "proved to be a most accomplished though somewhat eccentric gentleman" to whom everyone became much attached.   Awkward but ever jolly, he was a source of great amusement in the home, the camp, and in the field.[9]   Commissioned an "honorary captain" in the Confederate cavalry,[10] he participated in the battles of Chancellorsville and Brandy Station and, at Lee's request, accompanied the Army of Northern Virginia on its invasion of Pennsylvania.

Meantime, in addition to the Prussian Captain Scheibert, four other foreigners had joined the headquarters staff of the Southern army—Frank Vizetelly, artist and correspondent for the *Illustrated London News;* Lieutenant-Colonel Arthur J. Lyon Fremantle of the English Coldstream Guards; Francis C. Lawley, correspondent for the London *Times;* and Captain Fitzgerald Ross of the Imperial Austrian Hussars.   Each found a cordial reception at Lee's and Stuart's headquarters, as had Scheibert.   (Regrettably, the sixth European, Heros von Borcke, could not be with them.[11] He had been wounded a few days before at the Battle of Aldie.)[12]

---

[8] *Memoirs of the Confederate War for Independence* (London and Edinburgh, 1866), II, 202. See also *Mit Schwert und Feder*, pp. 43-55, 64-73, 343.

[9] *War Years with Jeb Stuart* (New York, 1945), pp. 203, 206-209. A very fine summary of the conviviality of this group may be seen in Mrs. Burton Harrison, *Recollections Grave and Gay* (New York, 1911), pp. 129ff.

[10] The same experience befell Frank Vizetelly, who was commissioned "honorary Captain" at Chickamauga by Longstreet. See Wm. Stanley Hoole, *Vizetelly Covers the Confederacy*, Confederate Centennial Studies, No. 4 (Tuscaloosa, 1957), p. 104.

[11] Every one of these six foreigners—Scheibert, Borcke, Lawley, Vizetelly, Fremantle, and Ross—later described his experiences in the Confederacy and it is fascinating to compare their several versions of the events. In 1863 Scheibert was 32 years old, Borcke 28, Lawley 38, Vizetelly 33, Fremantle 28, and Ross about 30.

[12] *Mit Schwert und Feder*, p. 135.

On the morning of July 2 Scheibert selected a very tall
nut tree on top of Seminary Ridge as the best point from
which to observe the impending Battle of Gettysburg. Soon
Fremantle and Lawley came along, armed with a long tele-
scope, and, as the battle began, the three men climbed the
same tree the better to follow with their glasses the movement of the armies in the valley.[13]   Generals Lee, Hill,
Longstreet, and Hood stood on the ground beneath them,
frequently calling up for reports on what the foreigners
could see. Lee talked freely with Scheibert, once saying,
"Captain, I do everything in my power to make my plans
as perfect as possible, and to bring the troops upon the field
of battle; the rest must be done by my generals and their
troops, trusting to Providence for victory."[14]   Throughout
the fight Scheibert "did not move a step from the tree."
He was convinced that he was "the only man on the
Southern side who could see everything going on in that
battle. . . ."[15]

After helping the Confederate Engineer Corps build a
bridge across the Potomac (thus "greatly facilitating" the
retreat of Lee's army),[16] in mid-July Scheibert returned to
Richmond, where he again met Lawley, Ross,[17] and Borcke
who, still suffering from his wounds, was able to join his
friends in their recreations.

Scheibert, having been deprived of visiting Vicksburg,
spent several hours studying the siege plans in the office
of the Confederate Engineer Corps—"without obtaining

[13] See "Letter from General John B. Hood," *SHSP,* IV, 147 (Oct.,
1877); and *Von Achten der Letzte. Amerikanische Kriegsbilder aus
der Südarmee des Generals Robert E. Lee* . . . (Wiesbaden, 1871),
pp. 142-143.
[14] "Letters from Maj. Scheibert, of the Prussian Royal Engineers,"
SHSP, V, 90-91 (Jan.-Feb., 1877). See Freeman, IV, 168 and below,
Chap. V, n. 20.
[15] See Fremantle, *Three Months in the Southern States, April-June,
1863* (Mobile, 1864), pp. 129ff. Lawley's description is in the London
Times, Aug. 18, 1863. (An edition of Lawley's contributions to the
Times is now being prepared for publication as a number in the
Confederate Centennial Studies.) See also Freeman, III, 107-134.
[16] Lonn, pp. 452-453.
[17] Fitzgerald Ross, *A Visit to the Cities and Camps of the Confederate States* (London, 1865), pp. 50, 103-104.

thereby any especially note-worthy information."[18] He also
revisited Secretary Seddon and called on Secretary of War
Judah P. Benjamin, but by far his "most interesting" experience was his conference with Jefferson Davis, who
asked him to seek an audience with Emperor Napoleon on
behalf of the Confederacy:

If the Emperor will free me from the blockade [Davis
said] and he will be able to do that with a stroke of the pen,
I guarantee him possession of Mexico. We forced this state
into submission in the year of 1842 [sic] with about 12,000
men since our soldiers are accustomed to the climate and to
the opponent's method of combat. We can still do that at
any time, for the dispatching of a corps of some 12,000 to
20,000 men would by no means be difficult for us in return
for the advantages of lifting the blockade, which is gnawing
at our vital nerve.[19]

Scheibert promised Davis that he would do all within his
power to help.

At five o'clock on Thursday morning, August 8, Captain
Ross and Captain Scheibert "took the cars" for Charleston,
where they again fell in with Frank Vizetelly.[20] There the
three foreigners shared many interesting and amusing experiences,[21] particularly those caused by shells from the
"Swamp Angel," a mighty Federal cannon which contin-
ually threw "Greek fire" into the streets.[22]

Vizetelly and Ross left Charleston for Chattanooga on
September 14 and shortly thereafter Scheibert took the train
for Wilmington. He spent a week there, inspecting fortifications, fishing, and sailboating in the company of "two

[18] Nevertheless, Scheibert wrote *Das Zusammenwirken der Armee
und Marine* . . . twenty-seven years later, a volume which evidenced
his academic but keen appraisal of amphibious warfare.
[19] *Mit Schwert und Feder*, p. 154.
[20] Hoole, pp. 85ff.
[21] Ross, pp. 118-120.
[22] Vizetelly's sketch and story appeared in *Illustrated London News*,
XLIII, 561-574 (Dec. 5, 1863) and in *Harper's Weekly* (New York),
VIII, 28 (Jan. 9, 1864) ; see also Hoole, p. 91. Vizetelly's remarkable
essay, "Charleston Under Fire," was published in *Cornhill Magazine*,
X, 90-110 (July, 1864).

beautiful Carolina women." Toward the end of the month he sailed for Liverpool, which he reached in late October, after having been delayed in Bermuda and Nova Scotia.

Upon his arrival in Europe, Scheibert, now a confirmed Confederate, hastened to Paris in hopes of somehow personally delivering President Davis' plea to Emperor Napoleon, but before he could "make all the diplomatic arrangements," Prince von Radziwill recalled him to Prussia.[23] Immediately, Scheibert was ordered to report his observations on the American Civil War, to discuss his views and findings with various Prussian leaders, and to lecture before military organizations.[24] In early 1864 he participated in the Austro-Prussian invasion of Schleswig as a member of Field Marshal von Wrangel's staff; in 1866 he fought in the Seven Weeks' War in Bohemia with General von Moltke, who "had learned golden lessons from the American Civil War. . ." (doubtless from Scheibert) ; and on August 6, 1870, during the Franco-Prussian War, Scheibert was thrice so badly wounded at the Battle of Wörth as to be evacuated to his homeland.[25] Between 1870 and 1878, now as Major Scheibert, he spent several months recuperating at the castle of General Vogel von Falckenstein, after which he served as post engineer at Posen, Minden, Cüstrin, and other places. In the mid-1870's he traveled to Tirol, seeking a cure for his wounds.

Meantime, Scheibert's interest in the military became more and more academic. In 1878 he resigned his active status in the Prussian Royal Engineer Corps and thereafter devoted his talents and time to military lecturing and authorship. The year before he had contributed an essay on General Robert E. Lee to the *Jahrbücher für die deutsche*

---

[23] *Mit Schwert und Feder*, pp. 154ff. For Scheibert's eulogy on Davis, largely a translation of an address by John W. Daniel, see *SHSP*, XIX, 406-416 (Dec., 1891).

[24] *Mit Schwert und Feder*, pp. 45ff. At the conclusion of one of Scheibert's lectures before 800 Prussian officers, according to Col. C. S. Venable, the audience stood and "gave three cheers for General Lee" (*SHSP*, IV, 89, Aug., 1877).

[25] *Die grosse Reiterschlacht . . .* , pp. 178; W. L. Langer (ed.), *Encyclopedia of World History* (Boston, 1948), p. 683.

Armee and Marine (Berlin), the first of many he was to
write about his famous Confederate friends.[26] Meanwhile,
he kept up a correspondence with his friend, Colonel Venable, and other Confederates,[27] in 1877 entering into a
heated controversy over the Battle of Gettysburg, which
was published in *Southern Historical Society Papers*.[28]
Indeed, by 1881 he was "proud to write" that he and Heros
von Borcke had "brought it about that in the German-
Prussian Army nothing concerning the civil war in America
is so in fashion as accounts of the deeds of Southrons. . . .
Lee, Jackson, and Stuart are now the favorite heroes of our
officers."[29]

Although Scheibert enjoyed other literary interests, he
seems ever to have returned to his experiences in America,
always stressing the importance and influence of the conflict
on European armies. As the years passed, he clung to his
theories, even though other German militarists turned their
attention elsewhere. Finally, his recollections became hazy
and his outlook increasingly nostalgic. He often resorted
to quotations, translations, and revisions, and his later
works are, therefore, often thin, lustreless, or just plain
"mixed up," as the Major himself learned to recognize.[30]

At the age of seventy-one, in 1902, Scheibert completed
the last book of his long and active life, appropriately, his
autobiography. Entitled *Mit Schwert und Feder* . . . , it
proved to be repetitious and contradictory. For example,

[26] See Bibliography, pp. 160-162, for a partial listing of Scheibert's
articles in *Jahrbücher* . . . , 1875-1892, and *SHSP*, XVIII, 423-428
(Dec., 1890), for an English translation of one of his essays.
[27] Venable's review of the French edition of *Der Bürgerkrieg* . . .
(*ibid.*, IV, 88-91, Aug., 1877) states that it would "make an admirable text-book for West Point or the Virginia Military Academy."
Luvaas, XXI, 113, n. 41 (Fall, 1957), points out a letter Scheibert
wrote Jan. 25, 1880 to John P. Nicholson in which he wrote, "You
would oblige me very much by giving me some hints about new or
important publications about the war."
[28] V, 90-93 (Jan.-Feb., 1877).
[29] *Ibid.*, IX, 570-572 (Dec., 1881). In this letter, dated Hirschberg,
Prussia, 13 Oct., 1881, Scheibert, lists some twenty-odd books and
articles from *SHSP* which he personally had translated into English.
See also J. G. Rosengarten, *German Soldiers in the Wars of the United
States* (Philadelphia, 1886), pp. 76-77.
[30] See Luvaas, XXI, 112-113, n. 38 (Fall, 1957).

much of the section covering his experiences with the Confederate States Army was copied verbatim from *Sieben Monate in den Rebellen Staaten*, which had been written thirty-four years previously, while the blood and sweat of battle were still fresh in his mind.

In 1904 Major Justus Scheibert, formerly of the Royal Prussian Engineer Corps, soldier, author, lecturer, teacher, and editor, died at the age of seventy-three, and was buried in Berlin.[31]

As a historian of the American Civil War Scheibert was thorough, keenly analytical, and generally correct, as time has proved. He was, as Jay Luvaas has stated, "one of the first European soldiers to understand the special characteristics of the Civil War armies." Unquestionably, he saw as much, if not more, actual combat than did any other European observer (Heros von Borcke can scarcely be called an "observer"). And his experiences, coupled with his long and serious study of the subject, rendered him "the most competent foreign authority on the Army of Northern Virginia, and . . . the only foreign observer to make a special study of the tactics of all three arms."[32] Indeed, as Luvaas has written elsewhere, Scheibert "wrote more about the Civil War than any other contemporary foreign military observer save perhaps Lord Wolseley." And such commentators as the more widely known G. F. R. Henderson, who curiously "never once in all his writings does mention Scheibert," quoted him directly and otherwise reflected the same "views expressed earlier by Scheibert."[33]

But, withal, one must recognize the Major's undeniable partiality towards the Confederate States of America. If

[31] Stanislaw Badony, director of the Miejska Biblioteka Publiczna, Szczecin, Poland, was unable to supply any data on Scheibert, and the American Embassy, Warsaw, Poland has advised that no information is available in the libraries of that city (see letters to the writer, Szczecin, Apr. 3 and Warsaw, Apr. 12, 1957, in University of Alabama Library).
[32] Luvaas' splendid summary of Scheibert's ability as an observer and critic of the American Civil War (XXI, 113-116, Fall, 1957) renders needless on the part of this writer any attempt to do likewise.
[33] *The Civil War: A Soldier's View* . . . (Chicago, 1958), pp. 108, 157.

ever there was a foreign Rebel, he was one! Throughout his
life he praised his old friends Lee, Stuart, and Jackson,
extolling their soldierly and personal merits and pointing
out the many benefits to be derived from a study of their
strategies and tactics. Yet, as a student of the American
Bürgerkrieg his approach was not unrealistic. In 1884, for
example, writing for the *Jahrbücher* . . . on "The Last
Days of the Rebellion. . . ," he presented these sound reasons why "the war on the other side of the Ocean" should
be studied again and again:

That war is interesting not only because of the significant
accomplishments of the cavalry, the first use of armored
ships, the heavy rifled artillery, the greater application of
technical science in war, the colossal development in sani-
tary methods; it will also remain for centuries an inex-
haustible mine for the soldiers who see in the din of war
more than mathematical combinations of battalions and
squadrons.[34]

In making this book I have become indebted to many
people, but I am especially grateful to Professor Alexander
C. Niven, formerly of Washington University (St. Louis),
who, himself engaged in translating and editing *Sieben
Monate* . . . , graciously yielded me the right-of-way. To
Jay Luvaas, of Allegheny College, I am also beholden. He
too was toying with the idea of an English edition of Scheibert's work, but, upon hearing of my interest in it, turned
his attention elsewhere. I shall never forget the generous
spirit of these two gentlemen-scholars.

I am also grateful to my colleague, Professor Joseph C.
Hayes, chairman of the German Department, University of
Alabama, not only for his translation, but also for his advice,
patience, and friendship.

University of Alabama   W.S.H.
August, 1958

---

[34] "Die letzten Tage der Rebellion; Aus dem Tagebuche eines
Kanoniers," *Jahrbücher* . . . , LI, 60 (July, 1884); Luvaas, XXI, 117
(Fall, 1957).

SEVEN MONTHS IN THE REBEL STATES
DURING THE NORTH AMERICAN WAR, 1863

CHAPTER I

Outward Bound

THE CIVIL WAR had already been raging for two years in the United States of America when, at the beginning of February, 1863, I left Berlin for a trip across the ocean to witness the battles and to observe the innovations of the Americans. I first went to London to ask the well-known agent of the late Confederate States, Mr. [James M.] Mason, for letters of introduction to influential men of the Southern States, and to get advice as to the way by which I might enter the South, which was blockaded on all sides. Both requests were courteously granted, and Charleston, South Carolina, was suggested as my destination. My interests also drew me to that place, since I intended to be present there at the impending siege.

In consequence of the travel instructions that were given me, I embarked at Liverpool on February 15 to go by way of New York to New Nassau (on New Providence, one of the Bahama Islands), from whence I intended to reach Charleston on one of the blockade-running steamers.

With anxious expectations, I began the voyage on the excellent steamer *Africa* (Captain Moodie), which took us to New York by way of Queenstown after a stormy voyage, for we were at sea almost fifteen days instead of ten.

Even on the voyage, which is interesting only on the romantic Irish Sea, with the steep, red cliffs of Ireland and Western England, as well as the green, foaming sea and the lovely landscapes of the coasts, I learned through personal observation in association with the passengers the deep hatred that divided the Northerners and the Southerners, that is, the Federalists and the Confederates. For in the boredom of the monotonous voyage, which was interrupted by general seasickness in a manner not exactly pleasant, political topics composed the sole subject of conversation, naturally only within sharply defined groups which formed in various places on the spacious deck.

The few Southerners, who knew that they would be in enemy hands in New York within a short time, carried on a furtive and restrained conversation, while the Unionists, feeling themselves on secure ground, engaged in loud and provocative discourses. It was my privilege, as one who was completely neutral, to take part in the sessions of both parties, since I naturally concealed my intention to go to the South. Not until the close of my voyage did I reveal my destination to a trustworthy, rich German merchant, Mr. C., who had an import business in New York, so that I might have in this large, strange city someone who could help me to some extent with advice and information.

As far as the Englishmen on board were concerned, I made the observation that the officers of the army, as well as those of the navy, sympathized strongly with the Confederates, while the struggle in America seemed to stir the industrial Britisher only so far as his material interests were at stake.

We finally entered the splendid harbor of New York, which, protected by well-armed masonry and earthen forts, gave a presentiment of the prevailing war, while life in the harbor and in the city itself breathed with deepest peace and showed lively industrial activity. Only the recruits and volunteers who were moving out to the parade, as well as the large signboards of the recruiting offices, which praised in the most glaring manner and with usual American pretentious publicity the regiments that were to be formed and their commanders, gently reminded one here and there that he was living in a land where a grim, fratricidal civil war was rending the most sacred bonds.

I used the few days that I spent in the world-famed

commercial city to become acquainted with the activity there and to see as much of the army as possible. Naturally, the first sight of the poorly disciplined troops, who were completely unrestrained in their physical bearing, made such an unfavorable impression on a soldier of the standing army that I first had to get completely accustomed to the idea of having before me a young army which was drilled only for war against similarly trained elements. So much the more warlike were the conversations that were heard here and there, and the more martial the battle reports that "our own correspondents" gave in the columns of the forbearing newspapers.

I had become suspect by registering for the passenger steamer *H.*, which was to carry us to New Nassau, the notorious smuggling harbor for the blockade runners, and only to the timely warning of Mr. C., who had been my faithful guide in New York, did I owe the fact that I was able on the night before the departure to transfer the letters of introduction from my room, where they were pasted behind the tapestry, to the ship lying in the middle of the Hudson, and to conceal them in the lining of a sofa. Thus, I was spared inconvenience, and perhaps long imprisonment, for on the next morning, on March 2, when I was about to go aboard, the secret police searched the passengers and even ransacked the ship itself for "suspicious" characters.

The crew of this ship performed even more vital services for a Mr. G., who was carrying important dispatches from London to the South, for the stokers hid him behind the coal in the bunker, so that he was not discovered by the police.

The partisan groups that formed very quickly on the trip to the Bahama Islands showed a behavior opposite to that of the passengers on the voyage across the ocean, for the Southerners were predominant here, while the minority who sympathized with the Union behaved in a very quiet and retiring manner. The English crew of the ship also showed unconcealed aversion for the North American rival of Britain.

The heat, which increased day by day, the intensified shining of the sea, and the heightened blue of the Gulf Stream were signs that we were rapidly approaching the tropical zone, and indeed, after a beautiful trip lasting four days, we entered the harbor of New Nassau by lamplight on the evening of March 5, to awaken on the next morning in a tropical world in sight of a friendly city teaming with Negroes and clothed in palm trees.

The delight that every novice feels at first sight of nature in the southern regions, with pleasantly warm weather, with fantastically beautiful colors of sky and sea, with quite strange, magnificently luxurious vegetation, and with people of an entirely different physiognomy, is so natural that I shall even refrain from introducing the reader to this pleasure, which, after all, will remain the same for all time, while the year 1863 gave life and activity in New Nassau a quite peculiar character.

The blockade business had indeed attained full flower in this year. Fast steamers purchased in England and Scotland at any price carried on trade between the blockaded harbors of Charleston, Wilmington, New Orleans, and Mobile and the smuggling harbors of Havana, New Nassau and St. George's (in the Bermuda Islands), while sailing ships provided communication between Europe and the last mentioned places. Naturally, a stirring, colorful confusion of sailors, traders, agents, and swindlers predominated in the formerly unimportant commercial ports, while the Negro, who was free here, carried on his work slowly or sunned idly in the dirt, since he could easily earn the small amount of money needed for his modest existence. Money rolled lavishly in these harbors, for the blockade trade yielded an enormous profit, since the things that were smuggled in were sold for two or three times the normal price, while the exported goods, such as cotton, tobacco, resin, and the like, which lay useless in the South and were, therefore, hardly worth anything, brought a six to ten fold profit, so that a steamer that made one round trip not only paid for itself, but also made its owner a rich man.

The danger of blockade running lay in winding one's way through the ships of the blockade fleet at night, in the absence of moonlight (see map of Charleston, p. 129), and in finding one of the channels that lead into the harbor. These channels lead through sandbars lying from five to twelve feet beneath the surface of the water in a semi-circle before almost all of the harbors on the eastern shore of America. They can be recognized in the daytime by buoys and floats, and by alignments of beacon fires at night, or, in the absence of the fires as now during the war, they can be found only by use of the sounding line.

The steamer is lost if it runs so firmly aground in one of these sandbars, or false channels, which end in the middle of the bar, that it has not worked itself loose by dawn, and there remains nothing for the crew to do but to take refuge in the numerous auxilary boats and to take along with them as much of the valuable cargo as possible.

If the dangerous venture is to succeed, the captain must be cold-blooded, especially when the blockade fleet is being passed, and he must not accelerate, even under fire, until he is in a real channel. The ship is safe when he has found such a channel, for under the control of the pilot, who knows his environment at night as well as in the daytime, the ship now flies at high speed to its destination. No ship of the blockade fleet can match the speed of the slowest blockade runner, and all traces of the runner are soon lost in the dark night.

During my stay in New Nassau, I reviewed by friendly invitation of English officers the exercises of a "well-drilled" Negro regiment of Zouaves, who carried out drills in rushing and in the use of arms with great accuracy, smoothness, and energy. These soldiers serve only for the maintance of internal order in the islands.

Since I am a fatalist about many things, I booked passage on the twin-screw steamer *F[lora]* immediately upon my arrival in the Bahama Islands, because it was to be the first of the six or seven steamers there to leave port. The ship was of light draft and had a speed of about fourteen knots.

Like all blockade runners, it was about the size of a cricket, was painted a greenish white in order to be indistinguishable from the waves at night, and was provided with a smoke-consuming funnel, ("self-condenser"), so that no escaping spark could reveal the presence of the steamer to the enemy when it was fired with the finest English nutcoal.

I paid a hundred dollars for the privilege of lying between bales of merchandise on this ship, of drinking warm, dirty water, and of sharing the ship's frugal fare.

The captain, a short, stocky, gruff master, learned upon setting sail that Union cruisers were on the lookout to seize booty between Abaco and Eleuthera. Our steamer, therefore, was brought into safe concealment between two rocky islands during the night, and after it had picked us up from a small boat, it sailed with a Bahama pilot through the notorious Bahama Reefs (rocks, reefs, and surf), so that we sailed northward into the ocean between Eleuthera and San Salvador, where Columbus landed, as is well known. I observed with reverence the uninhabited, rocky island which hospitably received the first European, and from which I was now also going forth with palpitating heart to meet my destiny in the unknown continent.

We learned on the way that seventeen blockading ships were guarding the harbor of Charleston.

We cruised around on the ocean in the yawl for three days, and we were so tossed about by stormy weather that even the captain did not escape seasickness.

We were lying still on the calm ocean around mid-day before we were to break through the blockade. The captain and the first mate were making astronomical computations to estimate our position, but I could see by the resulting wrangling that their reckonings did not agree. Therefore, the captain lowered the plummet, found the depth to be thirty-one fathoms, cast a knowing look at the chart, pointed his finger at a place in the Gulf Stream, and said positively to the pilot, "We are right here!" The latter took the reprimand quietly, but with a skeptical shrug of his shoulders.

I commended my soul to God and my body to the fish, and prepared to sink my credentials, which were weighted with nails, as well as my sword, in order to stand forth in case of eventual capture as Sch., an ordinary man of private means, which the words of my passport indicated me to be.

At 6:30 o'clock, when night was falling, a pitch-black night, the ship, which was about forty miles from land, started out on the daring adventure. We could easily reach the shore in four hours. It became windy and foggy. The plummet was already being dropped from time to time to determine the distance to land. The captain and the pilot hurled curses and contentious words at one another and took a swallow from time to time. The plummet was supposed to find the entrance to the harbor, but cold blood and orientation were to be the pilots in darkness as black as a raven. It finally became so shallow that the pilot ordered a change of course. I went to the bridge, where the captain and the pilot were standing, and observed to my anxiety that both were drunk. Faint courage had been restored and strengthened by alcoholic spirits. But the dose seemed to be too strong, for the captain was cursing, and the pilot accused him of not being able to state whether he was fifty miles north of Charleston or fifty miles south. In spite of the nearness of the shore, the pilot could not recognize anything in the fog and the darkness. In short, nobody knew where we were. Nevertheless, we were racing along like the wind in our vessel with a draft of one and a half fathoms. Hanging in the swaying boat next to the lee-board, the man with the sounding line called, "Five fathoms, four fathoms, two fathoms," but the pilot's command, "Half speed," resounded too late, for at that instant we lurched so firmly aground under the lash of the waves that the ship rolled repeatedly on its keel. The ribs groaned and creaked, loose barrels and boxes rolled around, dishes clattered and fell, and the swaying crew held firmly to anything in reach. The engine was reversed immediately. It groaned and moaned under weighted valve, vigorously working first one propeller and then the other, and with the help of the tide, which came to our aid, it actually freed us from the dreadful sandbar after a half hour's work. All of us breathed sighs of relief, and with this warning we proceeded slowly and cautiously.

We had been under way only a few minutes when the lookout suddenly called, "Gunboat!" At the same moment a big gun boomed thirty paces to one side with a bright flash of light and sent a bombshell zooming right above us across the foredeck. "Full speed!" roared the startled captain, who disappeared from the bridge with the pilot. The helmsman let the wheel go. A few sailors, and particularly two blockade-running Jews, crept into their berths in mortal fear, like ostriches that bury their heads in the sand. For a moment I was standing alone on the bridge, and in order to calm the people, I called as coolly as was possible in the unusual situation, "Be calm. They can't hit us. After all, it's dark!" The shamed pilot immediately pulled himself together, came running up, and with a firm voice ordered a westward course, since he saw that the ship was rushing hither and thither at random. The helmsman, too, was quickly back at his position, and soon the ship was again on a fixed course. But the blockade fleet also showed that it was not idle, for hardly had the command been given when a rocket came down beside us, and an electric [sic] light, which let its searching rays sweep the sea in all directions, peered and squinted at us. Still, the enemy did not seem to see us in the prevailing fog, for the ominous flashes of cannon sent their thunderbolts first past our stern and later in all directions except toward us. The only bad thing was that we were still working our way across the shallow water at full speed like a wild beast under pursuit, for only gradually was everything successfully calmed to the extent that the order "Easy," indeed "Slow," was given, and the sounding began anew as we went on at moderate speed. We were aground in the middle of the banks every hour, and a brisk north wind caused the shining, foaming waves to drive against us with particular sharpness when we ran aground. The atmosphere on the ship was one of rare excitement. We searched vainly in this manner for perhaps two hours without finding the channel. During the entire time the drunken captain uttered the most horrible curses (fortunately my English was then not adequate to translate them), as a result of which the pilot, likewise not sober, was evidently in despair. Suddenly the captain raged at the pilot: "You're an . . . ! We must have sailed half way up and down America and should have been in the harbor ten times. You don't know your business, you . . . !" The man at whom he stormed murmured something about false reckoning, but the captain screamed, "To the east, to the east! I must get out of this d. . . . . blockade, or we are lost!" But hardly had we started out in this direction, when masts appeared against the dark sky, and again a fire rocket went hissing past us. "To the west, full speed!" the pilot now commanded in turn. "I'll try it again!"

The work began anew, with alternate grounding and fear of discovery by the enemy, and with continuous sounding and the monotonous call: "Two fathoms, three fathoms!" In short, everything was in a feverish excitement until fear again overcame the captain after a half hour's search, when he gave the command, "North by east! Full speed!" and was driving us again into the open jaws of the blockade fleet in order to escape from the net. At the same time, he went into the cabin with the pilot to take another look at the charts, or to peer into the cup, while the steamer was racing into the open sea at full speed and without benefit of pilot, for nobody dared take command. Then my patience snapped under the extreme tension, and trembling with rage, I got them both out of the cabin with "full speed" and shouted, "Gentlemen, you are not worth a charge of powder. At last, we are inside the blockade, and we must absolutely stay inside it!" I returned both the defiance and the threats of the captain in like measure and with so much the greater success, since the crew took a stand entirely on my side, partly because of rage against their drunken leader, and partly out of gratitude for my friendly persuasion at the time of the first shot. The pilot also agreed with me, happy to have someone who was a match for the snarling captain, and we felt our way westward until sandbars seemed to be everywhere about us, whereupon we cast anchor to wait for morning.

Nobody closed his eyes. The moon rose at 4:30 o'clock, but fog obscured all vision. At 5:30 o'clock the sun revealed nothing but grey upon grey until a colossus at our side gradually became visible through the mist.

A ship? No. Thank heavens, it was Fort Moultrie, at the entrance to the harbor, to which providence had graciously guided us. We hailed with fiery jubilation the Confederate flag, which likewise waved from our stern, and with a certain satisfaction we greeted the signal shot that resounded toward us from Fort Sumter. We had landed in Charleston!

But we did not go ashore without having previously enjoyed a humorous postlude to the gloomy night. In order to show the audience standing on the bulwark and the scornful crew on the ship who was really running the steamer, the captain, exhausted by the night and still not completely sober, stood in the wheelhouse and gave commands in a stentorian voice. But when he was near an old, unrigged Spanish brig that was lying at anchor, he confused the commands "starboard" and "larboard" and ground against the stern of the old vessel, so that he crushed four boats, wreaked violence on the wheelhouse, and completely smashed a rowboat that was floating calmly in the harbor. The humor lay in the contrast and had a striking effect.

It was March 15. I took only enough time to dress quickly and was with General [P. G. T.] Beauregard by 9:00 o'clock in the morning to offer him my services and to request his permission to look around in the fortress.

He received me with great friendliness as a volunteer on his staff and entrusted the arrangements for my tour to his adjutant, Mr. [Lieut.-Col. A. R.] Chisolm, a likable gentleman who performed this service with great readiness by placing rowboats, passes, and his own horse at my disposal, so that I was able to reconnoiter thoroughly the full circumference of the stronghold.[1]

Naturally, I was never permitted to copy the good maps in the office, but the exact location of the lines was of little influence in the following siege, for the defense consisted almost entirely of detached batteries and forts. Since I had copied a map of the harbor from a good navigation chart on the journey over, and had entered on it the positions of the batteries with my good pocket compass, I was for the moment sufficiently provided with material to be able to follow the siege.

I also carefully probed the approaches and thoroughly inspected Fort Sumter and Fort Wagner, where I observed every detail that could have any influence on the defense.

I may say in advance that I did not find much that was new or instructive with respect to artillery, but I came upon much in the way of fortifications that aroused great interest. The skillful layout of the artillery earthworks especially aroused my high admiration.

The City of Charleston, which had a population of 40,000 in time of peace and was one of the most active trade centers of the South, was now only sparsely inhabited, with its richer part to the southeast, next to the harbor, occupied almost exclusively by homeowners and a few Negroes. The beautiful houses, therefore, which were picturesquely surrounded by verandas and enclosed in well-kept gardens, were standing lifeless and lonely on the streets, while only the older gentlemen of the civil population assembled in the hotel—the younger men were serving in the army—to discuss politics and the war.

These gentlemen in their black, formal suits and white, old-fashioned high collars, in their good-natured conversation and somewhat ceremonious manner, reminded me vividly of Old England's cavaliers, and not without reason, as I later learned, for here the ancient classical literature,

---

[1] *War of the Rebellion* . . . (Washington, 1880-1901), 1 series, I, 59 (hereinafter cited as *ORA*).

Shakespeare, Milton, and others were particularly cherished and abundantly fostered.

I also became acquainted with fellow countrymen, since the local German society invited me for an evening of entertainment, in the course of which they sang and performed a play. I was especially interested in the German preacher, who had studied in Berlin and had been living in the South for a long time.[2] He acquainted me with many characteristic customs and institutions of the South during our interesting conversation, and especially did he give me thorough information about the slave question, information which was based upon wide personal observation and which I later found to be generally accurate. Although Charleston was very interesting at that time, the prospect of a siege seemed to be so far removed that I decided to get closer to the important struggles that were threatening to break out on the northern and western boundaries of the Confederacy, especially since I had concluded my preliminary work in this stronghold.

Therefore, I secured space on the train to Richmond and became acquainted on this occasion with the railroad system of the South, which had at its disposal no shops for the manufacture of new locomotives or cars. Consequently, those on hand were repaired as well as possible with meager facilities and were "driven to death," as the people said. Naturally, the seats in the few coaches that were still on hand were frightfully crowded, and it might almost be considered punishment to sit or stand in the wobbly, jolting coaches for two nights and a day. A maximum speed of 12 miles ["2.5 deutsche Meilen"] an hour was established by law.

In view of the long supply lines on which the maintenance of the Southern armies was based, this state of affairs, which applied to almost all railroads of the South, naturally had a most adverse influence, about which we shall later become better informed.

[2] Lonn, p. 320, identifies the preacher as Rev. Louis Müller, pastor of St. Matthew's Lutheran Church.

After a long trip, I finally greeted with joy the City of Richmond, which lies picturesquely on the James River, on seven hills, like Rome, and in the midst of which rose majestically the "Capitol," where the Congress held its sessions.

The moral force of resistance was also centered in Richmond, the capital of the rebellion. Here was located not only the center of administration of an army that was almost too big for the people and their strength, but also the point of concentration of all army shops, powder factories, gun foundries, etc. The energy of the Confederate resistance that was typified in Richmond impressed me almost as much as the great efforts of the army later to hold the field against an overwhelming adversary.

The shops especially called forth my genuine admiration, for the South had previously had no large engineering works, or even arsenals, but only such shops as were able to keep the steamships and railroads operating. Nevertheless, it was possible as early as the fall of 1862 to procure in Richmond weapons of all types and munitions even in adequate quantities, to cast cannons of all calibers—Napoleon 12-pounders, rifled 3-pounders, 10- and 15-pounder columbiads, and rifled, breech-loading 7-pounders—and thus to be independent of foreign sources in case of emergency, which was extremely important in view of the trying circumstances of the blockade. In order to judge the difficulties with which the government had to struggle, the fact should be mentioned that even some of the machine tools first had to be brought through the blockade, others had to be manufactured, and the technicians for the most part had to be trained. The half-neglected mines were first reopened for the production of raw materials, and thus the ore for the cannons had to be procured and then transported to Richmond. Only on the spot can one appreciate the enormous energy and be amazed at the industry of a patriotic people in accord with their government and ready to follow it with devotion. Intelligence, unity, and the will to sacrifice brought forth such brilliant results.

They were even building a large foundry for 15-pounder columbiads this year, but when questioned, I expressed at the time my firm doubts about overdoing caliber in such a way, and these misgivings I later found to be substantiated.

I accepted with pleasure the friendly offer of Colonel [Jeremy F.] Gilmer, Chief Engineer, to lend me his horse for excursions if the occasion should arise, and I used the beautiful animal immediately to visit the famous battlefields around Richmond in company with Colonel [William P.] Smith and Captain [Henry T.] Douglas, both of whom were officers in the Corps of Engineers.[3]

I had a special urge to inspect these famous fields in detail because of the somewhat colored report of the French princes who had taken part in this campaign on McClellan's staff,[4] and because of other works. Unfortunately, I was not permitted to copy the unusually clear and fine photographs of the Office of Engineers.

In the early hours of the morning we rode to Mechanicsville, in the course of which we had to cross the dark Chickahominy, which was flowing along sleepily in the broad valley, flooding to a breadth of about two hundred to three hundred paces the low meadows with their highly picturesque groups of trees, just as it had done at the time of the battles.

The two gentlemen, who had fought in the battles (Smith on General Lee's staff), were kind guides and gave a clear commentary on the battles at noteworthy places on the field. The land north of the Chickahominy, on which the battlefields of Mechanicsville (June 26), Gaines's Mill, and Cold Harbor ["Cool Harbour"] (June 27) are located, rises in gentle waves about eighty to a hundred twenty feet above

[3] *ORA*, 1 series, XXVII, pt. 2, 350, 361; XXIII, pt. 2, 909; Freeman, I, 643; and James L. Nichols, *Confederate Engineers*, Confederate Centennial Studies, No. 5 (Tuscaloosa, 1957).

[4] Prince de Joinville, son of King Louis Phillipe, and his two nephews, the Count de Paris and the Duc de Chartres, sons of Duc d'Orleans, were commissioned "honorary captains" by President Lincoln in September, 1861 and assigned to McClellan's staff as aides-de-camp. See Francis T. Miller (ed.), *Photographic History of the Civil War* (New York, 1911), I, 115, 117.

the valley of the aforementioned river. The hills descend steeply only in the direction toward the river and toward several runs which cut deeply through the terrain in a direction perpendicular to the Chickahominy. These runs ("creeks"), Beaver Dam, Powhite, and Goodley-Hoole, repeatedly afforded the Unionists the opportunity for extraordinary defensive positions in the course of the battles.

Here there is inevitably forced upon the observer an admiration for the bravery of the Southerners, who, although in the minority, drove the superior enemy back from position to position in seven days of battle on this terrain which is so unusually favorable for the defensive.

Although almost a year had passed since this land had been the scene of battle, the whole country still looked as if it had been sown with debris—knapsacks, articles of leather, and broken weapons—while unpleasant miasmata lay over the deserted landscape. Only grunting swine wandered around on the level ground, often rooting at the shallow graves and gnawing on bodies which stared with distorted, horrible expressions at persons who rode by. Where was the time in those days to bury the many thousands of dead deep enough?[5]

After the scenes of battle had been shown to me with expressions of greatest admiration for the heroes Lee and Jackson, we rode on over the so-called Yankee bridges, which led like pole roads from 500 to 600 paces across the meadows and marshes of the Chickahominy, which is broader here, and returned by way of Savage Station and Seven Pines, where battles had been fought on June 29 and May 31.

On the following day I called upon the Secretary of War, Mr. James A. Seddon, who was almost overwhelmed with work, and whom I was never fortunate enough to see before eleven o'clock in the evening, since his duties were so heavy. We talked in detail about the military system, etc., and I received a short, but kind letter of introduction to General R. E. Lee. Although I intended to attach myself to the

[5] See Freeman, II, 108ff.

Tennessee Army, especially since it was generally believed that the conflict would be fought to a conclusion there, and also because I had good letters of introduction to General Joseph E. ["J.O.E."] Johnston, I decided, nevertheless, first to visit the Army of Northern Virginia encamped at Fredericksburg. Therefore, I took the train on April 8, after my pass had been approved, and again I found a little standing-room in the overcrowded cars.

CHAPTER II

The Army and the War Situation in 1863

THE QUARTERMASTERS, analogous to our supply officers, but also in command of columns on the march, had set up their supply depots at Hamilton's Crossing, a station near the Rappahannock and approximately in the center of the Confederate camp, where Colonel Smith from Richmond, now detailed to General Lee's staff, went with me to get a miserable mule cart that took us and our packs (weighing not more than twenty pounds in my case) up and down hills, over streams and logs and stumps to a little spot in the woods where five small, quite plain cavalry tents with attached chimneys were grouped around a Confederate flag.

Smith, an officer who was well-liked for his kindness, introduced me to the members of the staff, with whom I was to remain many months, contrary to my expectations, and to enjoy the most stirring, and thus the finest days of my life.

General Lee was lying ill in a farmhouse,[1] but in response to the letter of reference that I transmitted to him, he sent me a truly friendly invitation to consider his tent my own, together with the disheartening request that I remain at his headquarters only until he could get acquainted with me, and until I had seen the army, and that I then seek other lodging.

---

[1] Lee had fallen ill in late March, 1863 and was now at Yerby's farmhouse under doctors' care (*ibid.*, II, 502-503).

Major [Charles S.] Venable, a former professor of astronomy who had studied in Berlin and in Heidelberg,[2] brought me this news with the remark that I should not take it amiss, since this was such a serious war and the general had refused lodging at his headquarters even for the correspondent of the [London] *Times*, who was so esteemed by all, and who wrote very favorably for the South.[3] Since I soon became aware of the fact that the principal battles of this year were to take place on the Rappahannock, and since I did not have a second letter of introduction to anyone in this army, about which I knew nothing, I was at first quite dejected, but I made use of the short period of my stay to learn as much as possible about the infantry, which was encamped near us.

The army, which was recruited by universal conscription extending from the sixteenth to the forty-fifth year, made a very strange impression in its outward appearance, since nothing in the way of uniformity was to be seen, for everyone wore whatever he could get, or whatever his wife wove for him at home.

Also the extremely strict discipline on duty, on marches, and during the battles was definitely not to be seen in camp life. For example, nobody considered it an instance of insubordination at the time of the snow in April, when every stranger who passed through the camp, whether a general or a private soldier, was pelted with snowballs by the Texans, high-spirited as they were, though nonetheless renowned for their valor.

The army was divided as the European armies are, but numbers were no longer determinative after the many bloody battles. The companies consisted of about seventy-five to a hundred men. Two to four companies formed a battalion, and three or four battalions (usually ten companies) a regiment with about 1,000 men. Three to five

---

[2] Major (later Col.) Venable, one of Lee's aides-de-camp, had studied in Bonn and spoke German (*ibid.*, I, 641-642; II, 235, 403). See below, Chapter V, n. 1.

[3] The correspondent was Francis C. Lawley (see below, Chapter V, n. 7).

regiments formed a brigade, two to four brigades a division, and three to five divisions a corps, which was the smallest unit with mixed arms, and which ordinarily had a total strength of 20,000 to 30,000 men.

Cavalry in numbers commensurate to the circumstances was detailed to the corps for every special campaign or major action.

Artillery was likewise detailed to the corps according to circumstances, but every infantry or cavalry brigade was inseparably accompanied by a battery of four guns.

The infantry was armed with rifled muzzle-loaders, mostly Minié rifles, but one brigade had smoothbore guns by request, because the trajectory was flatter.

In my opinion the cavalry had a saber that was too light, while one squadron in each regiment was generally still armed with carbines in order to be able to fight dismounted as sharpshooters, so that the cavalry would not be defenseless against infantry.

The artillery had the most prized smoothbore 12-pounders (Napoleons), which composed perhaps two-thirds of the field artillery, and rifled 3-pounders, which were very accurate, to be sure, but of too small a caliber. It is to be noted that the rifled field guns were rarely ever able to make use of their great accuracy in the wooded terrain.

In addition to the 12-pounder Napoleon, the cavalry also carried the 6-pounder, rifled Whitworth ["Withwort"].

There was diligent drilling in the camps according to an old French drill manual that had been revised by [Brig. Gen. Wm. J.] Hardee,[4] and I observed on the drill field only linear formations, wheeling out into open columns, wheeling in and marching up into a line, marching in line, open column marching, marching by sections, and marching in file. (No hollow squares.)

The march proceeded at a slow stride of from eighty to ninety paces a minute, or on the "double quick," a slow trot.

---

[4] *Rifle and Infantry Tactics* . . . (Mobile, 1861, 1863).

The tactical unit in battle seemed to be the brigade. The drilling, according to my observation, seemed to be somewhat awkward. The cavalry drilled in a manner similar to ours, and the main emphasis was on a good jog, with loud yelling and shouting.

The infantry also used this sound, the famous rebel yell, in bayonet attacks.

The soldiers usually lived in groups of ten in tents or huts, to which crude chimneys were attached, a style of lodging which is extremely practical. On the one hand, the heat of the fire, which is dissipated in open bivouac fires, is held together, warms the cabin, and serves at the same time for the cooking of food. The fire also purifies the air in the tents extraordinarily well, so that these chimneys, which are a baked composition of wood and sod or clay, were highly favorable to the health of the army.

The staff used the time for extensive reconnaissance along the Rappahannock, in which I gladly joined, and by means of which I gradually got to know the inner life of the Confederate Army.

Interesting was the traffic between the outposts of the two sides, who had dug in about a hundred feet apart on the two banks of the Rappahannock, and who, in spite of their hatred, indulged undisturbed in fishing and barter and traded tobacco for tea and coffee, whereby vessels a foot long, carved from bark and provided with sails and helm, took over the transportation without further steering or piloting.

Also I learned to know the roads, the condition of which is evidenced by the fact that mules which had drowned in the roads, and whose cadavers hardly extended above the muddy water, showed the depth of the water holes.

In the brief period of my stay, I learned to like the members of the staff, and also General Lee, who visited his headquarters one day as a convalescent. I was introduced to him, and I observed with respect and pleasure the tall, handsome sexagenarian with snow-white hair and with dark, beneficent eyes, which had a look of kindness for every human being.[5]   With awe I beheld the victor of the seven great battles before Richmond, of Fredericksburg, and Sharpsburg, so much the more because he had formerly been an officer of engineers, like me. He commanded a cavalry regiment just before the war. He had distinguished himself as an engineer in the campaign against Mexico in 1842 [sic]. In his high top boots, his simple coat, his big felt hat, and with his modest bearing, far from all formality, since he wore his saber only on the march, he made the impression not of a soldier, but of a man of affairs.

As the time approached when I was to take regretful leave of headquarters, there came riding into headquarters one day a tall, stately major with plumed hat, high boots, and big gauntlets, to whom I was introduced without understanding his name.

Only from the conversation did I learn that he knew Pomeranian, and when I asked his name in surprise, he told me that he was von Borcke, that he had formerly been a member of the Prussian guardcuirassiers, and was later in the 2nd [sic] Dragoon Regiment.[6]   My joy over the acquaintance was naturally great, since I had so unexpectedly found a fellow countryman in a foreign land. He asked me to visit General Stuart, who happened to be in the vicinity on business.   On the very next day I rode out, full of expectation, to meet face to face the world-renowned, bold cavalry general, who was not to live to see the defeat of his people. In a simple tent, which also seemed to be his office, I found a young man in his thirties, with bold, flashing eyes and full beard, who looked very well in his gray jacket with the insignia of a general, and in gray trousers tucked in his high boots. He greeted me with frank and noble propriety, bidding me especially welcome as a Prussian.

---

[5] Lonn, p. 371, states: "Probably no more thoughtful act of hospitality could be found in the annals of war" than the ill General's warm reception of this foreign stranger. (Born in 1807, Lee was only 56 in 1863).

[6] In his *Memoirs* . . . (II, 201) Borcke confirms this first meeting with Scheibert. See below, Chapter II, n. 10.

Pointing to von Borcke, he said: "If you have any more like him over there, send them all over here!"[7]

I got along very well in general as a "Prussian," while the "Germans" do not by any means play the leading role in America.

When I took leave, General Stuart invited me to pay him a long visit at his headquarters near Culpeper. I accepted the invitation with great pleasure, for with him I had again found accommodations in the Army of Northern Virginia, and to be sure, accommodations that were quite welcome to me.

Before I left, Major Venable was kind enough to accompany me to the neighboring battlefield at Fredericksburg, and not only to tell me about the progress of the battle, but also to escort me into every nook where any part of this famous and bloody drama had been played. At that time the battlefield was still untouched,[8] but graves of the Unionists, who had been buried by their own countrymen, made a repulsive impression, inasmuch as the half-buried, half-covered corpses glared out of the sand with distorted features, often with both hands out of the soil and with fists clenched as if to utter a curse.

Fredericksburg itself was a heap of ruins, in which our outposts lodged as well as possible, and where they had constructed zigzags in the gardens as protection against enemy fire, in order to be able to get to the line of outposts without danger from pickets.

Every Sunday there was divine service in the vicinity of headquarters, which the General and his staff never missed.

The magnificent forest served as a temple. In a depression stood a table as a pulpit, around which from 500 to 600 earnest, weather-beaten faces silently and reverently listened to the truly spiritual and consoling words of the

---

[7] Lonn, pp. 171-175, stresses Borcke's ability, charm, and wit, adding that he possessed "many of the same qualities which made his superior officer, General J. E. B. Stuart, so romantic a soldier. . . ."

[8] The Battle of Fredericksburg had been fought four months before, Dec. 13-15, 1862. For some idea of the carnage referred to by Scheibert, see Miller (ed.), II, 123.

fine pastor, who conducted service in a simple coat and high riding boots, exhorting the people to perseverance, bravery and manliness. The pastor's name was Dr. [B. T.] Lacy, one of General Jackson's most intimate friends.[9]

I can not forget the fervor and power of his sermons. Numerous ladies in simple dresses had come to the divine service (on horseback, as always in this section), and were seated in an open half-tent. I saw a man seated on a log in the midst of the warriors, a fine, delicate, characteristic face, around which flowed a full, jet-black, curly beard, and which, under a simple military cap, betrayed devoted reverence. While I had my eyes fixed on this interesting phenomenon, Venable whispered in my ear, "Captain, that's Old Jackson!" That was the famous hero, Stonewall, respected by friend and foe alike.

The people spent Sunday very quietly, according to the English custom, not even playing the generally liked game of chess, at which I, moreover, was always beaten, which gave General Lee occasion for much teasing.

The conversation usually turned to politics, to conditions in the nation, and to the army, whereby the general desire for peace was expressed, but only after the liberation of the Southern States, and to an abhorrence of plundering, vengeance, or retribution for wrongs that had been sustained. I soon had a feeling of indescribable ease, as if at home in this absorbing circle.

I remained at General Lee's headquarters until April 19, when I departed after a reluctant farewell, and going by way of Richmond to re-equip myself there from my extra trunk, I went to Culpeper (Fairfax), whither General Stuart had transferred his headquarters and where he had invited me to visit him.[10] When I arrived in his camp a

---

[9] Rev. Lacy, an "earnest and eloquent" chaplain, was with Jackson, when he died a few weeks later (Freeman, II, 560-563). See also J. Wm. Jones, *Christ in the Camp* . . . (Richmond, 1887), pp. 298ff.

[10] Borcke, II, 201, thus describes this meeting: "On the 21st I had an agreeable surprise in a visit from a fellow-countryman, Captain Scheibert of the Prussian engineers. . . . My tent and its comforts, sadly curtailed however by the results of the heavy rains, . . . were gladly shared with my visitor. . . . [We] now suffered from the daily

few days later, the young General was sitting bareheaded and alone by a campfire and was singing with a clear voice a song that he had composed, the refrain of which was [sic] :

> Bully Boys juchhé, Bully Boys juchhé,
> will you see joy (Freude), join the cavalry,
> join the cavalry, etc.

The men answered with similar verses from the opposite hill, but with the turn of phrase, "will you see hell (Hölle), join the etc.," [sic] which led to a merry exchange of song and immediately made a cheerful impression on me. The General received me cordially and greeted Major von Borcke very obligingly. For any expedition that might materialize, the latter placed at my disposal a black horse, "Old Black," which, in spite of its jaded condition, its age, and its wretched appearance—one could count all of its ribs—was still a campaign horse the like of which I have rarely seen. I stayed with von Borcke in a round tent that had holes in it like a sieve—it was the only one of its type in the army—in the middle of which a puddle formed every morning, around which we had to creep carefully with bowed heads in order not to get wet. In free hours we would ride out on the hunt, Borcke on a beautiful white mule (Katy), an extremely funny animal that is well-known as an oddity and is capable of extraordinary work, but we never saw anything that was worth killing. Often he would read to me from his exciting diary, which he published in England. In view of the fact that I was having to lead a dull and quiet life at that time, I could only envy the author as I listened to his sketches of his varied adventures and active war experiences.

Stuart held Borcke in very high esteem and said proudly to me as the young man was walking around with splendid soldierly bearing, "A splendid, proud fellow!" He was

irruptions upon our camp of pigs exploring and devouring every thing that fell under their snouts. Not seldom, indeed, these intruders had the impudence to break into my tent in the middle of the night, having set their fancy on a pair of large cavalry boots of mine, which once or twice they succeeded in dragging far into the woods. . . ."

honored with the same epithet by every private cavalryman, all of whom knew him personally and liked to talk about his deeds.[11] I took advantage of the time in the camp and of Borcke's friendship to become acquainted with the cavalry of the Southern army. None will dispute the important role that the cavalry played in the American Civil War, and still, a brigade could be drawn up only at very few places there. Fences six feet in height cut through the woods and enclose every field, so that cattle grazing on the open range in the forests are kept away from the arable land. The woods, which easily make up five-sixths of the area near the Rappahannock, are filled with underbrush. The streams must be forded, indeed, they must be swum at some places in time of high water. Deep ravines even stop individual horsemen, and the roads themselves are in such a condition at certain times that cavalry movements had to be restricted to the thoroughfares. One can see the great importance that large bodies of cavalry have, even now, if he considers the significant results of General Stuart's bold raids and attacks, which forced the Northerners to form large cavalry corps, though contrary to their disposition.

The Confederate cavalry was divided into four quite distinct classes, the functions of which differed completely, which is responsible for the fact that an entirely erroneous idea about the Southern cavalry is frequently encountered in Europe, where the various types are confused.

1. *Regular Cavalry.* Combined into regiments, brigades, and divisions for skirmishes, battles, and raids in force. Stuart's, Van Dorn's, and Morgan's cavalry belong in this group. 2. *Partisan Rangers.* A kind of free corps that was not limited with respect to numbers. Their raids under a well-known commander (Mosby is the most famous one) are the most adventurous and the most stirring events of recent times. Their pay was their booty, which they were

---

[11] Lonn, p. 172, emphasizes Borcke's popularity, not only with his comrades, but also with the ladies. She quotes Mrs. Burton Harrison (pp. 130ff.) as reporting that Borcke once waxed enthusiastic over a Confederate belle by saying, "Ach, she was most beautiful in von home-spun dress and von self-made hat."

required to sell to the War Department at a fair price.
3. *Scouts.* Drawn mostly from the Indian states of the West,
they acted on their own responsibility. They had to be in
enemy territory from time to time and to report on all
movements of the enemy. They usually rode through the
outposts at night and hid in the daytime in dense thickets
or in houses occupied by Southern sympathizers. They
always had to be in uniform, and they differed from spies
in this respect. 4. *Couriers.* Young, skilled, nimble horsemen on excellent mounts performed orderly service and
were attached to headquarters, so that the commanding
general had sixty, a corps twelve, a division six, and a
brigade three, each ready for duty.

I noticed that there was a mysterious restlessness in the
air on April 28.[12] General Stuart received a number of
messages, dispatched couriers, and had a pensive look. I
had to get busy and make a small copy of a large map, and
everyone in the camp was more or less occupied.

Suddenly at daybreak, five o'clock, the General called into
the tent, "Gentlemen, everyone will be in the saddle in a
quarter of a hour!"[13] He invited me at the same time to
take part in the operations and appointed me captain of
cavalry on his staff, with the remark that I should put the
insignia on in order that I might be exchanged in case of
my capture. "For," he said, "they make short work of
civilians. A hastily convened court finds them quilty of
espionage, and they can thank their lucky stars if they are
not hanging from the limb of a pine tree on the very same
evening." Everybody whispered to me: "This is going to be
a big fight!" Borcke quickly gave me an old uniform, to
which I had to apply the insignia of a captain of cavalry
with my own hands. The staff had ridden away in the
meantime, nobody knew where. Although I galloped along

---

[12] Borcke, II, 202, states that he, Stuart, and Borcke had dined out
and that it "was in the night ere we reached our headquarters, . . .
little divining how soon we should be roused up again."
[13] *Ibid.,* II, 203. Borcke says Stuart called at "about three in the
morning," adding that the General "had just received intelligence that
the enemy were approaching the river at several points with a strong
force . . . and that we must hasten to the front without delay."

not more than ten minutes behind them, I was able to follow their tracks for a distance of only about 2,000 feet, when they became mixed with those of the regiments and were later completely lost on the pavement of Culpeper. While I was wandering around there, searching and asking questions, I experienced a remarkably pleasant minor adventure. Six pretty little girls from four to eight years old called to me entreatingly, "Halt," and, probably thinking that I was Stuart, they decked me and my horse with garlands of roses, which I later faithfully handed over to the General.

I first rode along after the wagon train, but fortunately I heard from a commandant of the quartermaster corps that the trains had been sent away in a direction opposite to the movement of the march. Therefore, I turned around, rode at random toward the Rappahannock, and actually had the pleasure of discovering the tracks of the General and of overtaking him at noon at Kelly's Ford. He was camping with his staff there on a hill, from which one would have been able to get a good view, if the forests everywhere along the river had not concealed the movements of the enemy. So far as I could learn, [Maj.-Gen. Joseph] Hooker was crossing the Rappahannock with his entire army in order to tempt Lee by a flanking movement to come out of his strong position at Fredericksburg, while [Maj.-Gen. John] Sedgwick was to carry on a holding action at the front. But in order to clarify the state of affairs, we shall take a look at the military situation of the moment.[14]

At the beginning of the year 1861, the Civil War, which had developed from apparently minor incidents and major fundamental causes, brought to arms two popular factions who were inexperienced with weapons and who had been devoting themselves exclusively to civil occupations. It seemed as if the lion's skin would be a poor fit for the domestic animals that were disguised in it. In the beginning, Europe's military circles followed the first somewhat disorderly clashes of the two champions with a smiling look,

[14] See Freeman, II, 508-524.

so much the more, since the North had only a few officers with a military education, despite the fact that the regular army was on its side. Such men had gone over to the South. On the other hand, there were in the South almost no private soldiers who had ever borne arms before the outbreak of the conflict. Boastful, swaggering bluster served for lack of discipline and order. After these preliminaries, therefore, the course of the first battle of considerable magnitude (Battle of Bull Run) could not fail to provoke scornful remarks and to awaken among military men the belief that the American War was not worth subjection to thorough observation. Therefore, it was followed only as a curiosity, but without profound interest.

The Battle of Bull Run, which was fought between the Rappahannock and the Potomac, as well as several other minor clashes in this region, had also shown the Americans that the waging of war would necessarily remain inconclusive without military organization, discipline, and training, and would cost more men, even with minor clashes, than would an orderly, energetic conduct of war on a large scale. Both sides, therefore, used the time from June (Battle of Bull Run) 1861, until the end of the year to organize their combat forces, service corps, hospital facilities, general staffs, etc., in order to be able to take the field with greater unity and effectiveness. The time passed with nothing but minor naval operations along the coast, in which ironclads played their first role, and wild, confused clashes in the West.

During this period of organization in the Southern army, with the unity of the nation, with the firm hand of a President trained in military affairs, with the military education of almost all Southern generals, which made the army a really unified and effective instrument in the hands of the commander, the transformation of an armed mob in the North into an organized army could only progress slowly and in an inadequate way. On the one hand, the President, who held supreme command without knowledge of military affairs, was not equal to the task. Furthermore, even the precarious position of the Union could not completely stifle inner dissension. And finally, jealousy among officers of high rank, as well as the democratic basis of an army that resisted discipline, paralyzed all fusing of the separate branches into a unit.

This brief sketch of the early development of the armies characterizes them and the manner of their conduct of war to the very end, but it is to be observed in this connection that the Northern army increased in military effectiveness through military experience in the course of the years.

Whatever one may think of his talents as a leader, [Major] General [H. B.] McClellan, an officer who was eduated at West Point, deserves the credit for transforming the Northern army into a force that was at least serviceable, despite all obstacles that were placed in his way. But in the spring of 1862, with his work still unfinished, and with an army that was still not an effective combat force, he attempted under the prodding of an impatient press to capture Richmond, the capital of the Confederacy, located on the peninsula between the James and the York Rivers, in the course of which the transport vessels accompanying him on the York River formed a good base of operations. The end of the expedition is well-known. After he had lost seven battles, after Stuart had burned all of his supplies and provisions in the rear in a bold raid, McClellan transferred his base (a word that has become proverbial in America and in England) from the York to the James River and was glad to escape to the Potomac with the remnants of his army.

The Confederate Army had been commanded by General Lee, who established here his fame as a field general. General Jackson had also had an opportunity to demonstrate the greatness of his military talent here, as well as on occasions that had immediately preceded. Prior to the events mentioned above, he had been ordered to hold his own with less than 20,000 men in the so-called Valley of Virginia, between the Potomac and the Rappahannock, far from the war theater around Richmond, against 80,000 men who beset him in three units, and if possible, to keep these troops from uniting with McClellan.

However, Jackson had not been satisfied with this purely defensive task, which was difficult within itself, but he had fallen like a lion upon the separate forces of each of his superior opponents and had so crushed all of them that they, taken aback, sought protection beyond the Alleghenies or beyond the Potomac. He had threatened Washington to the extent that the frightened government withdrew badly needed reserves from General McClellan to defend the capital city, and, leaving behind him the enemies that had been thrown into terror, he had finally hurried quickly southward on incredibly swift marches. He arrived thereby at Cold Harbor ["Cool Harbour"] just in time to fall so effectively upon McClellan's right flank in the Battle of Gaines's Mill ["Gaines Hill"] near Richmond, that the latter gave up further harassment of this capital city.

Now McClellan had also fallen into disfavor in the North, as had [Brig. Gen. Irvin] McDowell ["McDowall"] after the Battle of Bull Run, and a certain General [Maj.-Gen. John] Pope, who had penetrated with his unattached forces into the region between the Rappahannock and the Potomac evacuated by Jackson, was put in command. He was also supposed to gain laurels for himself, and he began by replacing the respectable waging of war introduced by McClellan with a brutal conduct of the business more pleasing to the mob. But the attempt failed completely, since he, circumvented by Jackson and attacked on the flank by the rest of the army, was sent home in such a fashion that he lost his glory and his office. The victorious Southern troops crossed the Potomac, and the worried Northern Cabinet again called McClellan to the colors, who was now given supreme command of the entire Northern army. At the Battle of Antietam (called the Battle of Sharpsburg by the Southerners), which was indecisive, to be sure, he succeeded in stopping the advance of the Confederates, who were already threatening Pennsylvania, but he was neither able to prevent the surprise of Harpers Ferry by Jackson, whereby the latter general captured a tremendous mass of war material and provisions, along with 12,000 prisoners, nor to disturb the withdrawal of Lee's army across the Potomac, since his troops were not able to undertake an operation so closely resembling an offensive after the battle mentioned above. General Stuart again succeeded not only in spreading fear and confusion in the rear of the hostile army in a cavalry operation carried out with rare boldness and energy, but he even outfitted his entire cavalry division with the booty and augmented it with 600 horses.

The failure of the campaign, which must be charged at least as much to the ineffectiveness of the Northern army as to the hesitant caution of General McClellan, became a basis for complaint against the General, who lost his command, however, mainly because of his moderate political tendencies, so that the command was transferred to General [Ambrose] Burnside.

The latter resolved, as they say, "to take the bull by the horns." He crossed the Rappahannock at Fredericksburg and made a frontal attack against General Lee's army, which was deployed concentrically on hills. This army remained strictly on the defensive, since the favorable terrain permitted a sustained fire of volleys almost everywhere from a depth of four lines, in addition to the artillery fire. The result was that Burnside's army, thoroughly staggered, made no further attempt to take the position at Fredericksburg after it had suffered losses seven times as heavy as those of its opponents. It was due only to the possibly excessive caution of General Lee, who had no knowledge of the demoralized condition of the beaten army, that the latter again reached the northern bank of the Rappahannock without being completely annihilated. (December, 1862.)

General Burnside shared the fate of his predecessors. He lost his command, which was taken over by General Hooker. The latter had made a name for himself by his personal bravery on the one hand, and by making serious charges against his predecessors and General McClellan on the other hand. He was called "Fighting Joe" by his friends, and he attempted to extol his fame in boastful talk and through a favorable press until the time also came for him to assume the role of action.

Because of the unserviceable roads, the swollen streams, and the unusually rough weather, the armies remained inactive during the winter of 1862-1863, confronting each other on the banks of the Rappahannock in the same positions that they had occupied before the Battle of Fredericksburg. That is where I found the army when I visited General Lee's headquarters in April, 1863. It consisted of Jackson's II corps, Longstreet's corps, and D. H. Hill's division .

The internal condition of the Southern army was by no means favorable at this time. The great crop failure of the year 1861 had forced the government to put the soldiers on half rations, soldiers who were already adequately supplied only with small grain, corn, and bacon, and it had become tactically impossible under these conditions to feed an army of 70,000 men at one and the same location. Therefore, not only D. H. Hill's division, but also a part of Longstreet's corps had been sent south to Richmond to facilitate the problem of provisions, so that General Lee's army probably numbered hardly 50,000 men. The Confederate cavalry was in an even worse condition. The lack of fodder, the rough season, and a disease that the cavalry had brought back from the North on the last expedition threatened to deal the mounted troops a mortal blow, so that after most of the brigades had been dispersed far into the country, General Stuart had with him only two very weak brigades, ([Gen.] Fitz Lee and [Maj.-Gen] W[illiam H.] Lee), whose horses, moreover, were in a very sad condition at this time.[15]

While the army south of the Rappahannock realized its weakness, the Northern army grew because of recruits that were arriving daily; and with its new uniforms, its ample number of new tents, and its adequate, even luxurious food

[15] The former was Lee's nephew, the latter his son "Rooney" (*ibid.*, II, 516, 420).

supply, it presented a remarkable contrast to the opposing forces, so that after the well-equipped Northern army, numbering upwards of 159,000 men, had passed in review before the President, it was labeled by the jubilant press as the "grandest army" under the sun.

With his 159,000 men, Hooker's problem was now to entice General Lee out of his strong position behind the Rappahannock. For that purpose he had contrived the following plan, the execution of which I was to witness:

He sent General Sedgwick across the Rappahannock at Fredericksburg with 45,000 men to hold the Confederate Army there at the front, while he himself, with about 109,000 men, crossed first the Rappahannock at Kelly's Ford, about forty-five miles upstream ["etwa 10 deutsche Meilen"], and then the Rapidan, to attack General Lee's flank, or, with Sedgwick pursuing him, to get him between two fires and to beat him, to destroy him, to annihilate him.

The enraptured Northern press was already celebrating victory and the downfall of the Rebels.

If General Hooker had carried out his plan as he had conceived it and had fallen like lightening upon the Army of Northern Virginia, the latter would have been in a very bad situation. But as we shall see later, Hooker pulled his strong army back upon Chancellorsville behind entrenchments and forfeited the initiative to General Lee, who exploited it to his advantage with his usual skill.

The Confederate Army consisted at most of 50,000 men in two corps commanded by Generals Stonewall Jackson and Longstreet. Each corps had three divisions: Jackson's Corps: A. P. Hill (later corps commander), Colston, Rodes; Longstreet's Corps: Anderson, McLaws, Early.

Only one brigade of Stuart's cavalry division (Fitz Lee) was involved in the fighting. W. Lee's brigade had special orders to the south, such as the protection of wagon trains, railroads, etc. It had no opportunity to go into action in the battle itself because of the broken terrain.

So far as artillery is concerned, there were probably twenty guns with the army.

According to official reports, the Northern army under Hooker numbered 159,000 men (compare Chesney, *American War*)[16] and included:

I Corps under Reynolds	VI Corps under Sedgwick
II Corps under Couch	XI Corps under Howard
III Corps under Sickles	(German Corps, earlier
V Corps under Meade	Sigel, later Schurz)
	XII Corps under Slocum

Most of these corps had a strength of three divisions, which contained four weak brigades. The brigades consisted of an irregular number of battalions, sometimes five or six, and seldom had a strength of more than 2,000 men.

General Lee, who had long been informed of the enemy's intention by scouts, reports of Northern newspapers, spies, etc., naturally would not be drawn into such an obvious trap, but he advanced slowly with 38,000 men upon General Hooker without getting too far from [Lieut.] General [Jubal] Early, whom he had left behind with 16,000 men to defend the position at Fredericksburg.

While Lee thus marched upon Hooker, Stuart was to observe the crossing of the enemy at Kelly's Ford, to accompany his advance with continual harassment, and to come simultaneously with him upon General Lee, whom he was to keep constantly informed of the enemy's movements. Since the enemy's army was always marching in thick woods, the task of the cavalry was by no means an easy one. How it was performed we shall see in the next chapter, where we shall again take up the thread of the story which we dropped on the Rappahannock at Kelly's Ford.

---

[16] C. C. Chesney, *Campaigns in Virginia, Maryland, etc. . . . .* (London, 1865), II, 209-216.

Battle of Chancellorsville

CHAPTER III

Battle of Chancellorsville

WHILE WE WERE ENCAMPED in the grass at Kelly's Ford, dropping the reins of our horses as always and letting them graze, couriers raced off to the front with reports and frequently returned with prisoners, who were thoroughly questioned. Among others, they brought along a Belgian officer attached to Hooker's general staff, who wanted to reconnoiter, and who, on his debut, had innocently mistaken our men for his own cavalry.[1]

We broke camp at four o'clock and marched parallel with the Army of the Potomac, which we could see clearly through openings in the forest. It was immediately greeted with several rounds from rifled cannon, which astonished the men and disturbed the march, for we could see the columns running hither and thither, although we learned from prisoners that no shot had hit. The longer we marched, the more prisoners came in, mostly stragglers who, panting under the burden of eight days' rations, had sought a safe spot to rest aside from the path of march. Our men had set out suddenly and without preparation, and thus the large ration of the enemy, crackers and bacon, was a real invigorant for them. When I also filled my stomach—it had had nothing since the previous evening—as well as my pocket with crackers that had been seized, I did not want to accept so much from the men who had gone out and got

---

[1] Borcke, II, 204-205, states that the Belgian protested vigorously against being considered a prisoner of war. Inasmuch as he was wearing a "Yankee uniform, no exception could be made in his case."

them, but they just laughed: "We'll catch some more Yankees," and they rode merrily away into the thicket.[2]

We rode on into the night, partly on bottomless roads that were difficult for the horse-artillery (smoothbore 12-pounders and, about half of it, rifled 6-pounder Whitworths ["Withworts"]), but it managed skillfully to get over the marshy places and to ford the romantic Rapidan at about 12:30 o'clock at night in chilly weather. The bank descended steeply to the river, about a hundred feet wide, which was murmuring along in the pale moonlight. The high, rocky bank could be seen rising majestically as a dark background beyond the river, while we could scarcely see the leading horseman or hear his splashing in the darkness and dead silence. Fortunately, he knew the ford and led us safely to the opposite side. Here we climbed steeply, abandoning ourselves completely to our tired horses. It was 1:30 o'clock when we moved into our much desired quarters, that is, we tied our horses in the pouring rain to a fence like those running through the woods everywhere, wrapped ourselves in blankets, laid our heads in our saddles, stretched out in the mud under the pine trees,[3] and slept as well as was possible in ironical illustration of the well-known song:

> And if I find no shelter,
> Then I'll stay at night
> Under the green trees,
> The little stars (?) [sic] will stand guard
> The linden in the wind will rock me gently to sleep,
> And at dawn the lark will wake me with her song.[4]

This time the lark was a blunt courier, who shook me: "Captain, the time has come." We got into our wet clothes

---

[2] *Ibid.*, II, 206. "The confusion and consternation caused amongst [the enemy] by this unexpected attack passes all description. . . . The road was covered with their dead and wounded, and sixty who had straggled off into the woods were taken prisoners."

[3] *Ibid.*, II, 207. Borcke identifies the place as Racoon's Ford. There the men, "cold, hungry, and uncomfortable," dismounted in the "wet and chilly" night, "a fine sleet drizzling," rested and fed their horses.

[4] Scheibert's version of the poem, given below, varies somewhat from

as well as we could and saddled our horses in the genuinely sad plight of having nothing but a little grass and a few grains of corn to offer them for breakfast. Indeed, on the previous day the animals had had to be satisfied with very sparse grass.

We continued the business of harassing the enemy on April 30 from early morning until far into the night, which could be done only on the side roads, where the artillery unlimbered its guns and fired into the columns, and where dismounted sharpshooters tried to cause confusion.[5] These tactics lacked the character of fool-hardiness only because the woods bordering the road everywhere were completely impenetrable. Otherwise, an infantry company would have been sufficient to disperse the cavalry column that was helpless against foot soldiers in this terrain and that extended a mile along the muddy, narrow road. All forward cross-roads were watched by small advance guards and flank detachments for the sake of greater security, so that the march was relatively safe.

As usual, Stuart rode on ahead with us when it began to get dark, since he, as an expert courier with good maps, was also the best scout.

Suddenly he stopped his horse and whispered in a low voice, "Things are not quite right up front! Major [Lewis F.] Tyrrell,[6] see what it is!" The latter rode forward cautiously and, after a few paces, fired six revolver shots up front. "All right!" said Stuart, riding to the rear after

the original of Emanuel Geibel, written in 1841, suggesting that he must have quoted it from memory:
> Und find' ich keine Herberg,
> So bleib ich zur Nacht
> Wohl unter grünen Baumen,
> Die Sternlein (?) [sic] halten Wacht.
> Die Linde im Winde, sie wiegt mich ein gemach,
> Und morgens weckt die Lerche mit ihrem Sang mich wach.

[5] Borcke, II, 207-208, states that the day was "just breaking" as they began the attack, which lasted off and on "until late in the evening." Then Stuart ordered his men "to turn off in the direction of Spotsylvania Court-house and go into bivouac about eight miles hence, at a place called Tod's Tavern."

[6] ORA, 1 series, 25, pt. 1, 58, 63; see also Blackford, pp. 91, 188; Borcke, II, 209.

he had called for cavalry. Since I had not noticed anything
in the darkness, either forward or to the flank—for the
senses and instinct become remarkably sharp only in the
course of a campaign—and could hear nothing but the
clatter of hard riding and of sabers, I lost my bearings
completely, and, frankly speaking, after some riding hither
and thither I no longer knew where friend or foe was.

I extricated myself from our cavalry, which had come up
in the meantime, and, evading the enemy horsemen as well,
I was glad when an acquaintance finally relieved me of my
uncertainty. The thrust of the cavalry that had been ordered
up lost its direction in the darkness and was turned aside,
and our horsemen came roaring back pell-mell in the woods.[7]
Annoyed, I let them rush by until a young friend nudged
my arm and said: "Come along with us. After all, you
can't whip the Yankees alone!" This also started me off
at the necessary pace, for we could already hear the pursuers raging at our heels. We were saved by a hard jump
over a rail fence, the top two feet of which had already been
taken off in the rush, for in the darkness the enemy cavalry
did not venture against the remnant of a fence that was
still more than three and a half feet high.

As soon as our regiment had crossed the fence, it slowed
down to a walk and immediately scoffed at itself in orderly
restraint. To my delight, I saw Stuart and his staff hurry
past us along the clearing, and I rejoined him.[8] In keeping
with Stuart's intention to bring up the reserves, we were
riding in a broad arc in the forest back to our road when
we heard a column moving along slowly in the dark. A
courier slipped forward cautiously and said in a low voice:
"Rebel!" "All right, Rebel," was the answer, and we were

[7] *Ibid.*, II, 208-211, explains that "about nightfall" Stuart, Scheibert and other decided to ride "about twelve miles distant" to visit
Lee's headquarters. He also verifies the surprise attack, the loss of
"a large number of our men and horses," and the "utter confusion"
and wild retreat of our "splendid regiment, which had distinguished
itself in so many battlefields. . . ."

[8] *Ibid.*, II, 212, also mentions a "tremendous fence" which at last gave
way "by dent of rider pressing on rider, and horse plunging against
horse." As he and his companions reached an open field, they came
upon Stuart and others who likewise "'had had wonderful escapes."

with our 2nd Regiment. With an exact indication of the direction, it was immediately sent forward to the attack, while the previously beaten regiment secured the flank. After confused noise and firing, we could tell by the Confederates' yells and hurrahs resounding through the dark woods that the barrier before us was broken and the way to Spotsylvania Court House was open. A horse was shot from under Major von Borcke during this attack.[9] We continued to ride along in the woods until about one o'clock, when we stopped to let our horses graze. Everybody retired except the outposts, and I also lay down in the rain next to a fence, wrapped in my blanket and worried as to how I was to feed my exhausted horse, for I could not find adequate provisions for it anywhere, and it was already beginning to fail me. On the same night, Stuart and several officers of his staff rode rested horses to General Lee's headquarters twelve miles away. When I was just about to go to sleep, a young lieutenant from General Fitz Lee's staff aroused me and invited me to accompany him to this General, who was to look after me by order of General Stuart, which he did with his now proverbial amiability.[10] Since everyone was expecting a battle, it was important for me to get near the main army in order to get a close view of the Southerners' method of combat. Therefore, I had them show me the direction in which I would find the main body of the army, which we had now approached, and when I came out of the splendid forest after an hour's ride, I had

[9] *Ibid.*, II, 214: ". . . I was met by a rider galloping toward me, who levelled a shot at me so close, the bullet passing through my hat, that I was completely blinded. Before I had quite recovered and could deliver my thrust, my adversary lost no time in firing his second shot, which entered the head of my brave bay, and stretched us both on the ground, myself under the horse. Luckily, however, I was able to disengage myself from the superincumbent weight of the dying animal; and, jumping up to look after my assailant, found that, fortunately for me, he had disappeared, without waiting to take advantage of my prostrate condition."

[10] Borcke accompanied Scheibert to Lee's headquarters. "I . . . rode on, with the untiring Stuart, eight miles further in the direction of Fredericksburg, to General R. E. Lee's headquarters, where we arrived just at daybreak, and I was enabled to snatch an hour's rest and tranquillity after all the excitement and fatigue of the night" (*ibid.*, II, 216).

the pleasure of finding several gentlemen of the headquarters staff busily drawing the infantry up in battle
order (in two lines and reserves). I stopped near General
R. E. Lee and joined in the advance. The fighting was quite
light, since the enemy evacuated position after position
after a few shots, putting the torch to the dry forests as he
abandoned them. But only the dry grass and the lower
twigs burned, so that it was possible to march through the
fire at most places. We stopped in a small clearing on a
hill (Aldrick). General Lee received the report that the
enemy had dug in strongly on the front near Chancellorsville and had secured himself with formidable, natural
abatis often 200 feet wide.

The General, therefore, set up his headquarters under
some trees at a place next to the road, where we stayed until
the following morning. The shrapnel disturbed us very
much here, for a rifled battery swept the road right next
to us and showered us thoroughly with fragments. In the
midst of the hail, I collected crackers for my hungry horse
from all packs of dead soldiers, which it devoured with
ravenous hunger, and I was thus able to offer the poor
beast at least some nourishment.

When I was just reaching for a pile of baked food that
had been spilled, a piece of shrapnel came whistling into it,
suddenly spraying the crackers in all directions, so that my
hand reached into an empty spot. The bombardment was
not unpleasant to me, for I was able to accustom myself
calmly to artillery fire, from which we were not to escape
within the next eight days.

When I returned to the tree where our staff was encamped
around the esteemed General, I saw this handsome, sexagenarian,[11] in a simple gray coat without insignia, waiting
by the tree trunk and peering thoughtfully into the distance,
as if he were expecting someone. After some time, a thin
man with black beard, black hair, and somewhat stooped
posture dismounted. In spite of his weather-beaten countenance, this man had features more like those of a thinker

[11] See above, Chap. II, n. 5.

than of a warrior. With an attitude of great respect, he approached the General, who shook hands with him in a manner that revealed sincere pleasure and esteem. The newcomer was the famous Stonewall Jackson. All eyes were turned with veneration and pride on the group, which had something of rare solemnity. The silence was broken only by the shrapnel, pieces of which went over us with monotonous whirring, sending down twigs and leaves.

Soon the two were involved in serious, eager conversation, which obviously ended in complete agreement, for in the evening sun the result was mirrored in the countenances of the friends, who were seated with averted faces by the tree trunk. They let their glances sweep afar and gave free rein to their winged thoughts. Lee, the old man, removed his hat after several minutes. Who can guess what was going on at this moment in this heart that was burdened with heavy responsibility, what was stirring in this soul that was filled with designs?

Jackson, stooped as always, with lowered head, showed mighty facial movements, in spite of his apparent calm. Almost simultaneously with his chief, he removed his cap from his curly head and extended his hand as if in prayer, reverently lifting up his handsome eyes. Then there was a whisper: "Look! Stonewall is praying as if in battle. That portends a bloody day." It is well-known that, when the battle seemed not to reach a decision, Jackson on his horse in the thickest rain of shot would often lift up his arms to heaven as if in prayer, apparently always with success. Soon the two generals rose. With calm countenances radiating hope, they shook hands again and again, as if the parting were ever so difficult, and for a long time each looked into the honest eyes of the other.

Jackson rode away.

I wonder whether the friends suspected that this would be their last handclasp.

The faithful Jackson was not to live to see the outrage against his land. His soul was to be spared this sorrow.

The spell was broken. Troops marched off in all directions, couriers delivered or went away to get dispatches, the fire of the skirmishers at the front increased in intensity, the staff closed in around the General, and the night covered everything with a thick veil. Everyone put his piece of waterproof cloth or piece of tent under himself to hold off the harmful evaporation from the ground and pulled his woolen blanket over his body. Thus camped general and private soldier.

Planters and planters' sons, who had formerly known only a life of pleasure and luxury, looked satisfied in spite of all this, since they had had no night's quarters other than open air and tent for three years, and for the most part they took out their prayer books in genuine Old English piety, following the consoling words especially worshipfully today, as on the eve of battle.

A friend of mine, a member of the staff, expressed the general feeling to me when he said: "There are going to be great events, and many a mother's son will embrace the grass! When those two men get together, history becomes pregnant and bears blood for us and hell for the Yankees!"

After he had done me the honor of introducing me to General Jackson before the latter rode off on that evening, General Lee gave me the gentle hint to stay with Stuart if I wanted to see anything. I do not remember the friendly, even gentle words that this general, usually a man of such brevity, spoke to me, since I could only watch the splendid eyes that were looking at me in the course of the conversation. But let us again take a look at the situation and at the map before we ride on. General Lee, who saw that he could not make a frontal attack with 35,000 men—for he had left 15,000 under Early to oppose Sedgwick with 45,000 men at Fredericksburg—against an enemy three times as strong, with over 100,000 men behind strong entrenchments, decided to send General Jackson with his corps (some 20,000 men) around Hooker's right flank to cause confusion, while he was engaging him on the front with 12,000 to 15,000 men. (See battle map [p. 53].)

Saturday, May 2

According to instructions, I rode out at five o'clock in the morning to join Stuart, who had set up his headquarters in a house near Catharine Furnace. Borcke approached me very seriously there and said: "Quiet, Captain. We are in deepest mourning. Our favorite Channing ["Chamming"] (Major Price), is dead. He bled to death last night." The beautiful daughter of the house was tearfully giving the last loving attention to the corpse, and the previously mentioned minister, Dr. Lacy, pronounced the final moving rites over the lifeless body of the youthful hero, whose voice with cheerful laughter and light conversation had often sustained our good humor by the camp fire.[12] Everybody was standing around disconcerted. Stuart, supporting his bearded head in his hands, could not avoid sobbing. During this scene, a courier made his way through the door with the words, "General Jackson wishes to see General Stuart!" The latter, as if awakened by a stroke of magic, quickly donned his hat with waving plumes and went with long strides toward Jackson, who was awaiting him on his horse, which, incidentally, was not famous for its beauty.

"What's the matter, Stuart? You look so disturbed."

"Channing is dead. A shell fragment opened his artery, and he bled to death before help could come."

"May God comfort you," said Jackson with sincere expression, "but come, I need your cavalry."

Thereupon the generals discussed the projected flanking march. The cavalry, to which the right flank of the enemy had become accustomed, was to conceal and cover the movement.

The columns of the II Corps were already coming up. General Jackson had his forward troops construct a bridge of wooden fences, brush, and earth across the swollen Poplar Run under his own supervision, and then he rode ahead with Stuart. In order to learn more about the security service of the local cavalry, and to look around in general, since I

---

[12] Blackford, p. 204, and Borcke, II, 220, also record the death of Major Price, Stuart's adjutant.

was already oriented, I rode ahead in the thick forest with
the forward troops and had the good fortune to be with
them several times when they made contact with the enemy,
who withdrew as soon as he caught sight of us. It was
likewise his cavalry that blocked the way from time to time.
As could be seen from the eager conversations accompanied
by lively gesticulations, and from the speed and diligence in
the execution of movements, the men of our corps were in
the business with body and soul, for after a long period of
inactivity. Old Jackson, who had never led his men into an
inglorious affair, was really on the move again.

The maneuver is marked on the map.[13]

At Wilderness Tavern, near Wilderness Run, the line of
battle was formed similar to that of Frederick the Great.
Two combat ranks, in long lines that maintained alignment
by brigades as well as possible in battle, had sharpshooters
about 250 paces before the front. [Maj.-Gen. R. E.] Rodes'
division formed the first line, [Brig-Gen. R. E.] Colston's
the second, and General A. P. Hill's constituted the reserves.
On the right flank, the Stonewall Brigade, which Jackson
himself formerly led, had the order to engage the enemy's
front.[14]

It was about four o'clock. As soon as a unit was posted,
the men would lie down very calmly, since everyone knew
that it was a question of quick envelopment. Consequently,
there was intense alertness, and all was so quiet that the
Union drum was heard beating time for the evening parade,
which was a matter for many jesting remarks. Nowhere
could one see more than eighty to a hundred paces in the
woods.

When all had been posted in battle order, the cavalry
before the front was removed, in a sense, the veil was lifted,
and the order to advance was given. The lines, anxiously

---

[13] The "famous flank march which, more than any other operation
of the war, proved the brilliant strategical talents of General Lee, and
the consumate ability of his lieutenant Stuart," is described in *ibid.*,
II, 223-224.

[14] See John Esten Cooke, *Life of Stonewall Jackson* . . . (New York,
1863), pp. 301-305.

holding their course in the woods and mutually correcting one another aloud, moved forward slowly and deliberately at first. Not until they encountered the startled enemy, who resisted them momentarily and fired musket and battery salvos, did the Confederates advance more briskly, not firing until they were close upon the enemy. The noise that now arose in the thick, echoing woods really defies description. Since that time I have been present at many big engagements, but I have never again heard such an infernal spectacle. No longer were single salvos heard, nor sporadic cannon shots, but a howling of fire arms in deep bass and high voice which surged and subsided like a somber melody, while shot and shrapnel whizzed through the air, causing leaves and twigs to rain down. In the meantime, none of us in the deep forest saw what was going on aside from us. Suddenly, there arose on all sides a loud outcry, the so-called rebel yell, which the Northerners feared so much. The firing diminished, and the Confederates now fell like lions upon the confused enemy, who, attacked by surprise, was not able to restore order. The first battalions were hurled back after brief resistance, and the regiments just fired another salvo and advanced, blocking the way of the troops following them. In vain the batteries sought space for a second mounting in the forest and had to drive away. The confusion became greater and greater, the roads—for only individual infantrymen could slip through the woods—became filled with the fleeing enemy, and the Rebels rushed after them. The wagons, batteries, and ammunition carts traveling beside the road were hindered in their flight by fences, so that the horses, deserted by their riders, wandered around in all directions or began to graze. When a large clearing (at Tady's Farm) permitted a view of some extent, my eyes beheld a remarkable sight. The Southerners, after the fleeing enemy, dealing ruin with shot and bayonet, though no longer in fixed order, were following with yells and at a fast pace upon the heels of the unfortunate corps formerly commanded by [Brig.-Gen. Franz] Sigel and now made up entirely of Germans.

All order in the enemy army seemed to have broken down, and the demoralization seemed to have reached its climax. Weapons, packs, coats, cartridge pouches, even jackets that were thrown away to facilitate running, covered the region. Artillery teams in harness were stalled by the fence, and a battery, deserted by everyone, stood on a height ready to fire. Indeed, open writing cases and pens still in inkstands next to them gave evidence of the suddeness of flight. In the midst of it all, the wounded were writhing or the dead were lying in various positions, just as their final movements had left them.

Only night brought an end to the pursuit, since friendly troops had unfortunately encountered one another in the unbelievably thickly overgrown, broken terrain, and it had become impossible to recognize anything at any considerable distance. General Jackson ordered that the engagement be called the Battle of the Wilderness, since the so-called Wilderness Run flowed along close to the battlefield.

Since I might possibly be accused at least of great partiality, in view of the numerous extenuating reports of the Northern press, which tried to soften discussion of this defeat, let me insert here in justification of myself a Unionist paper's description of the battle.[15]

. . . .

This was Jackson's last blow, and it really hit the mark!

Although darkness put an end to the pursuit, General Jackson still would not rest, for he was afraid that the Northern army concentrated at Chancellorsville, about 100,-000 men, would withdraw before the victorious arms of the Confederate troops numbering only a third as many, and he decided, therefore, to create fear and confusion in the rear of the enemy camp that night with a regiment of infantry and a like number of cavalrymen, in order to make the enemy believe that the envelopment extended that far. Therefore, Stuart advanced through the pitch-black forest perhaps more than half an hour in greatest secrecy with the

[15] The long quotation (here omitted) was translated by Scheibert from *ibid.*, pp. 252-253.

troops mentioned above—I accompanied him—and then he halted, whereby we had an interesting moment to observe the reserves of the Northern army unconcernedly cooking by a fire in the thicket.[16] Jackson had given the order to fire upon anyone who approached the front, especially upon cavalry. In the dark night he himself lost his bearings to some extent, emerged from the thicket, came unexpectedly upon his own men, and fell from his horse, his left arm pierced with three bullets by his own troops. His captain of engineers fell at his side mortally hit, two other gentlemen of the staff were wounded, and three couriers were either wounded or killed.[17] The frightened enemy fired into the momentary confusion. The General was borne away on an improvised stretcher on the shoulders of his men. But even this was not to be enough, for an unfortunate shot killed one of the bearers and again hurled the hero to the ground after a bullet had also smashed his right hand.

He asked that no announcement of his wounding be publicized and turned the command of his corps over to General Stuart. Not until the next morning did most of us learn about the frightful loss that the Southern army had sustained, although we were near the incident.

[16] Borcke, II, 227-229.
[17] *Ibid.*, II, 259ff. Cook, pp. 254ff., identifies the killed captain as J. K. Boswell and Col. Stapleton Crutchfield as the wounded officer. Capt. R. E. Wilbourn escaped injury and promptly reported the tragedy to Lee (Freeman, II, 533). Crutchfield recovered from his wounds and reported for duty in February, 1864, as this heretofore unpublished letter (in University of Alabama Library) from Lee to Col. Josiah Gorgas testifies:

Hd - qrs: 15 Feb. '64

Col

Col Crutchfield who was severely wounded at the battle of Chancellorsville has reported for duty. I do not think that he is able to do field duty yet awhile, without great risk, & therefore desire for him less laborious service. I have thought you might have such in the Ordnance Dept or around Richmond. Col Crutchfield since the beginning of the war, served with Genl Jackson, was selected by him as chief of Arty of his Corps, which position he held, when wounded. Will you please let me know whether you can give him employment if ordered to you.

I am with great respect
Your Obt. Srvt.
R. E. Lee
Genl.

But events roll on past life and death. Therefore, we shall leave the wounded General in the hands of his friends until a lull in the thunder of cannon gives us time to memorialize one of the most outstanding heroes of modern times and his enviable end.

It is interesting that the Federals had also attempted an envelopment of Lee's army on the same day, and indeed, down Louisa Run. They captured a battalion in the course of this attempt, and with more vigor they could have caused great trouble, but the news that Jackson had just passed them, and a fast march of [Lt.-Gen. Richard H.] Anderson's division, caused them to abandon the object of their attack and to withdraw again without having accomplished anything. (The maneuver is indicated on the map [p. 53]).[18]

When we returned from the little flanking maneuver that had had such mischievous results, there lay before us, quiet, but strewn with the rattling, the dying, and the dead, a battlefield on which the moon spread its gentle light, giving the scene a peculiarly solemn character. I rode over almost the entire field, since the first great battlefield that I had ever seen captivated me irresistibly. I felt my unfortunate inability to assist the disabled, but I noticed that a helpful hand was sitting by almost every wounded man. On the crest of a hill, the face of a young, fallen Unionist soldier—for hardly any others were left—attracted me in a singular way, a soldier who had the features of a young woman and a countenance so affable in death that I looked at it for a long time. It was unmistakably the face of a German.

Finally, I sought a place among the dead horses and men next to a cavalry outpost and was able to furnish my horse a decent meal of oats that I collected. One does not learn in time of peace what a joy it is finally to be able to give grain to a horse that he has ridden for five days, in the course of which it has been able to soothe its feverish ravenous hunger only in pauses and at night with scanty

[18] Borcke, II, 231-232; Freeman, II, 534. Stuart informed Borcke that "the attack was to be renewed at the earliest dawn of day . . . !"

grass and a few wretched crackers. When I picked up the
first sack of oats in the pursuit on this day and spread it
before the poor beast, it fell to its knees in order to be able
to eat faster and better, and it presented a spectacle such as
would perforce have moved a stone to pity.

Sunday, May 3

On the next morning I woke from a deathlike sleep. I did
not have time to clean up or to make sentimental observations about my surroundings, which were by no means
inviting, but instead, I had to get quickly into the saddle,
since everyone was already on the move, and as I observed,
all were moving toward the right.

Indeed, General Jackson's corps, now commanded by
Stuart, had won so much ground in the Battle of the
Wilderness that the army, that is, Jackson's and Longstreet's corps, could unite, if the former moved to the right
and the latter, under General Lee, moved to the left. (See
map [p. 53].)

I went out on horseback across our right flank to see how
the terrain before our front looked and to meet General Lee.
After I had ridden about an hour, I came upon a clearing,
in the middle of which was a Negro cabin. I had just put
my hand in my pocket to get a respectable coin and pay
hard cash for some grain, when I saw that several soldiers
were coming out of the house, and I was about to ask them
whether they had seen General Lee's corps. Suddenly I
realized to my great surprise that the men were Unionists,
for whom I seemed momentarily to be certain prey, for I
had nothing resembling arms except my dull saber. (I had
not had an opportunity to sharpen it.) Neither did I have
time to deliberate, and thus, Pomeranian that I am, I in-
stinctively snatched out my sword, impressive at least for
its size, rode firmly up to the men, and roared into the
resounding forest with a strong voice, "Surrender! You
are surrounded by cavalry!" I confused the astonished,
hestitant men completely with the equally loud call, "Down
with your weapons, or you are dead men!"—in bad English,
as I later heard—and had the comfortable feeling of having

the five men unarmed before my horse. Since I could only fear that the others in the house might shoot me down, I shouted back at random, before giving the command "March," "There are more of them in the house. We have counted all of them, and they will all be killed!" Turning away, I had gone just a few steps when a sixth one ran like mad from the house, about thirty steps away, and joined the sad procession. The men told me that they belonged to the 6th Ohio Volunteers, and that some of them were in the position painful, to be sure, of having periods of service that would have ended within a short time. After wandering around for a half hour in the dense woods on ways completely strange to me, I was honestly glad when I finally came upon a Southern regiment, which received me with a welcome when I related the imperative manner of my making the capture, while the duped enemy pulled long faces when they heard how they had been taken. General Lee and Stuart laughed heartily at the adventure. However insignificant this little incident was, it was still of value for my stay in the South, for from that time on, I can well say, I was really received with cordial friendliness and warmth by everyone. Since the anecdote had appeared in Southern papers, copied from the London *Times*, I also became well-known, which eased considerably my problem of getting to know the armies.[19]

The two Confederate corps joined on this morning in a hook forming a battle line, which is sketched on the map, as are the entrenchments and positions of the Northerners.

The plan was to attack the front of the enemy, who was indeed superior in numbers and was entrenched, but who was probably somewhat demoralized by the blow of the previous day.

[19] Scheibert's singlehanded capture of six Yankees with his sword is confirmed by Borcke (II, 244-245), who adds that "the gallant Prussian marched the whole six triumphantly back to General Lee, by whom he was highly complimented for his coolness and pluck." Freeman (II, 549) says that "Major von Borcke rode up presently [to Lee and Stuart who were seated at a little fire] and had to be told of the adventure that had befallen Captain Scheibert. . . ." Lawley's account is in the *Times*, June 11, 1863.

The Northerners, of course, had dug in again during the previous night, and indeed toward the south in trenches and about sixteen battery emplacements, which swept an open, sloping space about 300 to 400 paces wide. This entrenchment C had been joined to the earlier easterly one consisting mostly of large abatis. Again, Hooker had even had an extensive fortification laid out to the rear in order to take up a second, new position there in case of defeat. On the whole, up to that time in the war the Northerners had prepared everything from the outset for retreat and cover, and not without reason, for the Army of the Potomac could not boast of even a single decisive victory in the three years during which the war had been raging.

The Southerners on the contrary, bold and resolute as they were, seldom let the opportunity for spirited attack escape, and they almost always carried off the garland of victory on bayonet point. With the Northern army's hesitancy that waited things out, and with its lack of energetic leadership, they could always choose the favorable time and place to attack and seize the initiative.

A ride along the front had shown me that the decision lay on our left flank. Therefore, I joined its advance and was an immediate witness of the attack.

The Southern army advanced.

A roaring din arose again along the entire front at the first clash with the enemy. The first line, B, consisting of trenches, was taken in the initial attack.

Beyond this line, and separated from it by a ravine, rose the previously mentioned Hill C, crowned by about sixteen battery emplacements and by trenches which, with troops standing behind them, permitted firing from four lines. A well-swept hill ran down into a ravine on this side similarly as before the Duppel fieldworks. The first line, which was scattered somewhat by the murderous fire that covered Hill B, rallied in all calmness in this ravine to push up the hill of death.

No more frightful place can be imagined than the still completely intact position that was to be stormed, and I hardly dared believe in success. But the masses are moving and are marching slowly and deliberately up the open field.[20] The entire hill across the way becomes veiled in clouds, and grapeshot, as well as rapidly fired salvos, spray among the bold lines, making great gaps and leaving crowds of writhing people behind on the ground. The advance proceeds calmly. These veterans have already stormed similar positions around Richmond and in fifteen other battles. They do not break. But a second salvo and fire from four lines, from the trenches as well as by the men behind them, have too frightful an effect among the ranks. The attack begins to falter, the line of attack becomes serpentine, and the advance gradually changes into a withdrawal without much order. But the proud men walk down the hill in slow, calm steps, calling "Steady! Steady!" to one another in order not to become excited, else irreparable misfortune might result from lack of form and low discipline. From time to time one or the other calmly fires back. The men rally again in the small ravine and form a line. The mass, indignant at the withdrawal, moves forward again across the field already strewn with bodies; again it calmly withstands a salvo; but again the thin, broken line wavers and hesitates, about a hundred paces from the position, and again the gallant men, going back calmly with the vigorous call, "Steady," seek protection in the ravine.

Now help is summoned. General Lee sends as reinforcements the last remaining troops of the weak reserves, who have already had to help everywhere on the front. After a brief pause, the wonderful band of heroes, firm as a mass of iron and composed as stone, this time irresistible, advances again with resolute self-control and indomitable energy against the hill that is spewing trouble. The cannon spray death and destruction. Whole ranks are mowed down by the close salvos. Still, the cold bayonet's steady courage breaks the resistance of the Unionists firing safely behind

[20] The reader will note Scheibert's enthusiastic change from past to present progressive tense in his description of the Battle of Chancellorsville.

the ramparts, and with clear, victorious yells and shouts, the attackers now fall upon the wavering lines, raging frightfully with shot and bayonet thrusts among their adversaries.

Victory had also been won at other places when the men threaded their way through abatis that were poorly protected by trenches and fell suddenly upon the garrisons in the trenches.

Thus was stormed the first line, the capture of which was aided essentially by a battery of twenty guns posted on Hill A, which was so favorably placed that it enfiladed a part of the enemy trenches and the batteries on Hill C.

The Unionists effected a lodgment just one more time—in and around the buildings of Chancellorsville—but when they were smoked out, they pulled back completely into the second position.

Although the success of the first attack was now fully assured, there would soon be new work, for when the savage din of battle happened to pause briefly in the general relaxation of tension after the bloody action, we heard violent thunder of cannon to the rear on the Fredericksburg Road. It was evident that the Northerners under General Sedgwick, with a superior force of 45,000 men, had stormed the position opposite Fredericksburg (Marye's Heights), which General Early had defended with a rear guard of about 15,000 men, and that they were forcing him back, while he, in obedience to orders, was moving slowly toward us and defending position after position.

The moment was tense and critical. General Lee was undergoing a hard mental struggle as to whether, with his forces somewhat in disorder and exhausted by several days of fighting, but still effective, he should storm Hooker's second position despite all risks to the contrary, or go back with a part of his forces and help Early against Sedgwick— whether he should stake everything on a complete victory or win a small but certain advantage.

He chose the latter! He ordered the army remaining at Chancellorsville to dig in opposite the Northerners, and he himself moved with [Maj.-Gen. Lafayette] McLaws' and Anderson's divisions on the road toward Fredericksburg, partly on the very same night.[21]

On the morning of Monday, May 4, the General fell so vigorously with these troops upon the right flank of the unsuspecting Sedgwick—now engaged on the front with Early—that he retreated across the Rappahannock at Banks's Ford as fast as his men and horses could move and without putting up a real fight.

Early's, McLaws' and Anderson's divisions marched back to Chancellorsville on the fifth, and a general attack on the Northerners' camp was undertaken. But Hooker had already abandoned the position of his own accord on the previous night, and only stragglers and an abundance of camp equipment—tents and other military baggage—fell into the hands of the victors, all of whom were provided with a piece of tent material or waterproof cloth and were sheltered during the terrible weeks of rain that now followed, while the Northern army had to suffer considerably in the cold, stormy, rainy weather.

If the activities of the army within the past week are reviewed, one can only bestow highest praise, praise of sincere admiration, upon the commander and upon the army for its energy, activity, devotion, valor, and almost super-human achievements.

After this disclosure of the course of the battles, which were fought almost continuously in the darkness of the forest, I venture to return to my little experiences, which will perhaps give the picture some perspective here and there and will best give the reader an impression of events.

On Sunday morning, as has already been stated, I had witnessed the violent attack on Hill C while I was standing or lying among the trees at B, in the heavy shower of bullets,

[21] Borcke, II, 244, states that on the night of the 3rd he "found General Lee and Stuart seated by a small bivouac-fire discussing the day's events . . . and here, too, I found my Prussian friend Captain Scheibert, greatly elated over an adventure he had met with on the early part of the day [the capture of the six Federals], his original way of recounting which greatly amused us all."

and making a sketch of the assualt before my eyes in order to give permanence to the unforgettable impression. The trees next to me were in such a condition that one could not lay a hand anywhere on the bark without covering a bullet hole. Most of the trees were broken down and just raised their splintered remnants to the sky.

When I rode back to General Lee, full of excitement over my experiences, I found him standing next to the battery at A, described above, observing the progress of the battle through field glasses. Although he had sent his staff back somewhat because of the heavy fire, he kindly permitted me to remain at his side, and now for the first time I had an opportunity to observe the hero in battle.[22] No trace of excitement was portrayed on his gentle countenance. He received dispatches calmly and prepared a few orders just as quietly as usual. When I expressed frankly my admiration for the lion-like bravery of his men, he said: "Give me also Prussian discipline and Prussian forms, and you would see quite different results!" In the course of the conversation, in which he fervently deplored war and bloodshed as usual, he said that his chief aim was to keep the men morally disciplined and to guard against barbarism. "You see," he said, "here you have before you the elite of our people from sixteen to forty-five years of age. The state is to be made up of them in the future—*they* are later to pursue peaceful occupations and to practice quiet civic virtues. War is a savage business, and one must accustom the men as well as possible to self-control." The General carried on this conversation while the battle was in full fury, in the course of which he eagerly watched the progress of the fight through glasses.[23]

---

[22] In *Der Bürgerkrieg* . . . p. 39, Scheibert states that Lee told him, "I plan and work with all my might to bring the troops to the right place at the right time; with that I have done my duty. As soon as I order the troops forward into battle, I lay the fate of my army in the hands of God." Later, says Scheibert, Lee added (p. 181) that he tried to make his "plans as good as my human skill allows, but on the day of battle I lay the fate of my army in the hands of God; it is my generals' turn to perform their duty." See Freeman, II, 347.

[23] *Ibid.*, II, 538, IV, 217; Kaufman, p. 570; *Der Bürgerkrieg* . . . , p. 39.

While we were standing next to one another at that place, a Minié ball fell right before our feet and buried itself in the ground. General Lee picked it up and handed it to me with the words: "Captain, this was meant for one of us. Keep the little piece of lead as a souvenir of this day." No other token has made me happier until this very day.

Upon advancing farther, I also met Major von Borcke under heavy fire, to which Stuart had again recklessly exposed himself.

The sight of the battlefield was grandiose, which is understandable when one considers the fact that the losses on both sides ran up to more than 30,000 men on a small space. Horses and men were lying around in heaps, especially on Hill C., while the wounded in countless numbers writhed, were carried back, or hobbled back, often using their guns with upturned stocks as crutches. Still, one could only be astonished at the extraordinary organization of the medical service, for as early as ten or twelve hours after the battle, friend and foe were at least provided with water and the most urgent preliminary surgical dressings. In addition to the excellent management of the ambulances, the following factors helped essentially in promoting the care of the infirm: "On the one hand, the three years of war had made most of the men passable surgeons, at least for the first moment of injury. Furthermore, the extraordinary abundance of springs permitted the placing of the wounded along the brooks, where they were able to use an uninjured limb to get water from the brook for thirst and for burning wounds. And finally, the professionally trained practice of physicians, doctor's aids, and stretcher-bearers."[24]

Repeated instances of the great self-control of the wounded likewise elicited my admiration. The Confederates considered it a disgrace to groan or cry aloud with certain wounds (in the case of some, it is unavoidable), so that by listening to the groaning one could tell from afar where a

---

[24] This quotation is almost identical with that used by Scheibert in *Mit Schwert und Feder*, p. 103, and attributed to the chief surgeon of the Army of Northern Virginia.

Confederate or a Unionist hospital was located. A well-known officer came past me with one hand concealed in his hat. I asked: "Are you severely wounded?" "No, only the hand is gone, Captain!" A superior officer whose abdomen was in a frightful condition heard from the men who were bearing him on their shoulders that his regiment was passing. He raised himself painfully on his stretcher, and with friendly glances he waved to everyone. Only I, on horseback, could see how his deathly pale head sank back exhausted and distorted.

Reports of even more extraordinary traits were current in the army, but I am telling only what I saw with my own eyes. Let us return, however, to the main thread of events.

Generals R. E. Lee, Stuart, and the slightly wounded A. P. Hill set up their headquarters next to an apple tree near Fairview (Hill C), although this place was directly in the range of a rifled battery of the enemy's second position, which repeatedly forced us day and night to leave the field for a half hour. After twenty-four hours, this place was really harrowed by shrapnel, and the apple tree alone, next to which the General's tent of many pieces and patches was located, could show three direct hits and a number of scars caused by shell fragments.

Most of the Southerners were buried during the first night, while the Northerners and the dead horses mouldered on the field because of the continual engagements and the limited and exhausted forces.

These corpses looked frightful, turned black with time, became highly bloated, and spread a fearful odor that will certainly remain for life in the memory of those who camped six more days on the battlefield, as we did.

It was interesting to see the signs of joy in the army. There was no wild, wanton rejoicing celebrated by the firing of mortars, but a quiet shaking of hands with the cry that, thanks to heaven, this slogan, "On to Richmond," was also frustrated. To be sure, things were noisier at the campsites, where fresh meat and genuine Mocha (a priceless delicacy in the South) were substituted for hard crackers and cold bacon for the first time in a week, and the cold camp on the open field was exchanged for a warm tent and woolen blankets. The enemy had left so many supplies that our little army was fully provided with warm bedding. General activity, good natured jests, and a feeling of ease cheerfully greeted one everywhere. The army also outfitted itself as far as possible, with woolen clothing. I had time later to inspect the defensive works of the Northerners, who seemed to believe that they were safe behind any breastworks. Therefore, fence boards that were thrown together, with some dirt thrown over them, often took the place of shelters, and they frequently did more harm than good, for a great number of corpses and men wounded by splinters were often seen lying at those places where a small mortar ball, able at most to kill one man, had smashed through the wooden material. These wounds, moreover, are much more ghastly than bullet wounds, because the splinters have a lacerating and mangling effect.

On this day [May 7] General Lee issued his modest, dignified, pious Order Number 59, in which he gave God alone the glory for the victory and, far from all self-esteem and boasting, placed *his* merits in the background.[25]

On May 7 we rode in bad weather back to our old camp facing Fredericksburg, but it was located several thousand paces to the south, with a view of the picturesque Massaponax, which wound along at our feet, while oak trees and sassafras bushes between our tents afforded some shade, and the roots of the latter furnished material for a slightly sweetish but tasty tea.

This is perhaps the place to give a sketch of the provisioning at headquarters. Two meals, breakfast at seven in the morning in inactive periods, at four o'clock on marches, served in the mess tent (a piece of sailcloth which protected against sun and rain), and dinner at six o'clock in the evening, or taken after the march, constituted the highly practical method of feeding. The courses were simple, the same in the mornings as in the evenings: cornbread (bread

[25] *ORA*, 1 series, XXV, 805.

baked of maize) and wheatbread lay on the table, the latter often prepared as crackers. There was also coffee mixed with parched wheat or corn, and some tea, also sassafras tea, meat and molasses (a type of syrup cooked from sugarcane). Butter was a rare delicacy, as were eggs. Nevertheless, with the attendant hunger, never has a dinner tasted better than this simple food in pleasant company.

On many days there was naturally nothing but bacon and crackers, with which was drunk the splendid spring water that gushes forth, pure, cold, and silvery clear, every thousand steps in Virginia.

In camp life I also became better acquainted with the troops, who, in spite of hardships, in spite of the earnest disposition that the war aroused in the Southerners, were by no means averse to humor, which especially characterized the wild Texans. There have been published so many letters of private soldiers from the campaigns in Schleswig and Holstein, from Bohemia, from Italy, etc., to show the character and the spirit of the army, that there may be a place here for a note from a young member of the Stonewall Brigade which gives some idea of the innocuous camp humor of the Confederates. I translate it as literally as possible.[26]

. . . .

We left Old Stonewall in the story when he was being borne away from the tumult of the Wilderness, severely wounded. When the news of the wounding was brought to General Lee, he said: "Indeed, it is a pity, gentlemen; he has lost his left arm, but I have lost more, for I have lost my right!"[27]

General Lee sat down immediately and during the Battle of Chancellorsville wrote [his now] famous lines to his severely wounded friend: "Could I have directed events, I

[26] This long letter and a sketch of Jackson's early life (omitted here) may be seen in Cooke, pp. 14-15, 19-21ff., 220-223.
[27] Freeman, II, 560; see also R. L. Dabney, *Life and Campaigns of Lieut-Gen. Thomas J. Jackson* (New York and Richmond, 1866) p. 716, and Cooke, p. 271.

would have chosen for the good of the country to be disabled in your stead. . . ."[28]

I probably need not even mention what a feeling of confidence and respect for the leaders and what just pride these noble lines created in the army and in the people. They ran like wildfire from mouth to mouth. I myself was a witness of the sympathy that these words called forth.

Unfortunately, the initially good condition of the patient, who underwent an amputation soon after the wounding, grew considerably worse. An inflammation of the chest, probably also caused by the fall from the stretcher, made his condition serious. When this was reported to General Lee, the soul of this commander was most profoundly moved, and he, who could control every emotion, was not able to master his sorrow. "Jackson will not—he can not die!" said he with trembling voice,, "He can not die," and he gently averted all who would draw near him.

On Sunday, May 10, we went to divine service with General Lee, as was our custom. The previously mentioned Dr. Lacy held the divine service in the midst of the numerous tanned warriors in his usual, persuasive, impressive manner. Suddenly he rose. He had his text, "God turns all things to the good of those who believe in Him," and he said, "General Jackson, whom I left yesterday, gave me this text. *He* also cheerfully suffers his disability and considers himself fortunate in the loss of his arm, which he says has exalted his spirit more than any previous occurrence. In *his* case God has also turned the severe wound to the best. But, our gallant leader, children, hovers in greatest danger of being taken from us by death. Let us pray for him, that the Dear Lord God may sustain him for us."

Now there occurred an indescribably touching scene. All of the thousand warriors who were assembled in the quiet grove fell upon their knees with the sign of most earnest fervor and followed the moving words of the most stirring prayer by the dying general's pious friend, who besought

[28] *ORA*, 1 series, XXV, 769; Freeman, II, 543.

heaven to spare the life of this heroic heart for his native land, for the good of the South in war and in peace!

On the way home, I spoke with General Lee about the sermon, and he said: "But the doctor forgot the conclusion of the prayer: 'Thy will be done always.' The spirit of the noble Jackson will be with us, his example must sustain us. Indeed, he will still lead us, even though his body may be called away!"

The prayer of the many warriors, which was certainly echoed a thousandfold in the quiet tents, was in vain. Mrs. Jackson had to tell the general clearly and sincerely on Sunday morning that he must soon die. He answered: "Very well, very well; all is in order!"

His last words were: "A. P. Hill, prepare for action!"[29]

·   ·   ·   ·   ·   ·   ·   ·   ·   ·   ·   ·   ·

During my stay in the camp, General Lee ordered me to produce an impartial, true battle map of the battles at Chancellorsville, since the maps published up to that time by the Northerners had always been completely distorted in their favor.[30]

Therefore, I rode on the morning of May 6 to the battlefield almost four miles away. The odor would have led me to it from afar, even if I had not known the way well. The sight of the dead horses and unburied corpses corresponded to the stench. The signs of battle, now gruesome in decay, became more unpleasant, since, instead of vultures—for they were already satiated—Jews with harpy claws were plucking the last booty from the dead and from the field. I surveyed the place with my practical compass, which I always carried with me, visited on the way back the house where Major Price had died, and was received there in a very friendly manner. I learned here that the Northerners had come immediately after we rode away to the Battle of

[29] Following this quotation Scheibert inserted a eulogy (here omitted), copied from Cooke, pp. 7-8.
[30] Vizetelly later told Scheibert that this map was the only one made during the course of the battle and that he and other observers copied it for their own publication (*Mit Schwert und Feder*, p. 101).

the Wilderness, had acted like mad men, and had naturally turned everything upside down. On the same evening I rode back to our camp, where I remained several days.

But a cessation of movements had set in, and in other places the flame of war just continued to blaze. After many efforts in the West, the Northern army in General Grant's successful campaign had reached as far as Vicksburg on the Mississippi, where the Confederates had improvised rather extensive fortifications. Although the capture of this stronghold was for the time being not of far-reaching importance, still, some moral value had become attached to the possession of the place, the reasons for which I could not fathom, so that the existence of the West was even identified with its defense. Vicksburg was now under attack and was certainly being vigorously defended. Therefore, I as an engineer desired very much to be present within this stronghold, and so I took leave of my kind hosts and received many good wishes and letters of introduction for the trip.

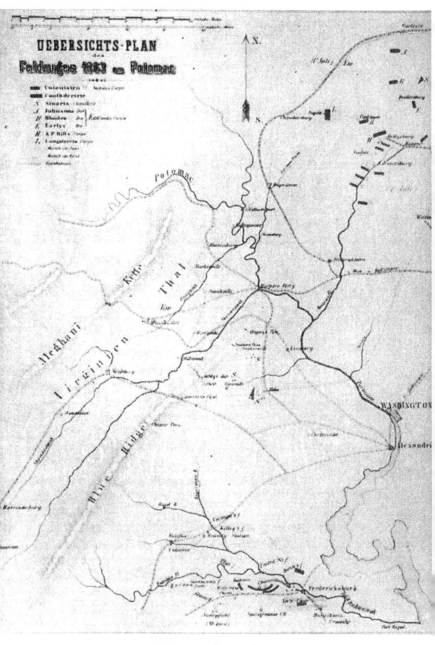

Potomac Campaign

CHAPTER IV

Cavalry Battle at Brandy Station

ON MAY 30 [10] I LEFT FOR RICHMOND, where I paid my respects to the President and to several cabinet members, and, in accordance with my commission, I drew in great haste the battle map of Chancellorsville, in a rather large corner of which I made a sketch of General Jackson encouraging his men. Indeed, I had made a sketch of him on the road three hours before he was wounded, unobserved, so I believed, until I saw that he turned away, blushing slightly and smiling. I sent the map to General Lee at his camp and later had the pleasure of receiving from him a very friendly letter of thanks in his own handwriting. I made full preparations in all possible haste to leave for Vicksburg on the fifteenth. But man proposes, and God disposes. A severe fever and dysentery forced me to bed, so that I could not be up and about. I was always dreaming in wild phantasies that I had returned to Europe without accomplishing my mission, without having seen Vicksburg, and I felt the greatest pangs of conscience for having been so negligent.

My attention in the confused and overcrowded hotel consisted only in the fact that a dull-witted Negro set the largest possible pitcher of water by my bed every morning. Otherwise, I lay all alone with my fever.

One day—it was my birthday [May 16]—Major von Borcke entered my room, unexpectedly, but to my great joy, and brought me an invitation to visit General Stuart. He said that an expedition of some magnitude was pending, probably to the North. I declined the invitation, since I intended to go to Vicksburg as soon as my strength would permit me even to creep along. "It is too late," said von Borcke, "Vicksburg is so completely surrounded by Grant that the boldest scouts succeed only with difficulty in getting information in." After he had shown me through authentic reports the absolute impossibility of getting there, I gladly accepted his proposal. If I had reached Vicksburg before the encirclement, as was my original intention, then I should have been captured with the entire garrison. I should have seen there neither an interesting defense nor a skillful attack, nor would I have experienced all that lay before me.

On May 21, as soon as I was able to shuffle along to some extent, I went by train to Culpeper, which lies at the foot of the Allegheny Mountains (Camp [Channing] Price). Here, in Stuart's camp, I recuperated in the splendid spring air, lying in the tent or on the grass in the sun, for standing and walking became very difficult for me, quicker than I might have expected. During the pause in activity, I had an opportunity to witness here two great reviews under General Stuart, one with over 9,000 horses, and one with over 12,000. The cavalry division was first drawn up and fronted, with ranks rather well dressed. General Stuart rode along the front with his staff in a long gallop and then rode back behind the line, whereby the men shouldered arms.[1]

Thereupon, the men marched past, first slowly and then in a gallop by squadrons. In the gallop, which they executed superbly and smartly, a shrill yell was uttered and sabers were bandished as in every attack. It was a genuine pleasure to see the skill and assurance with which the men managed their horses, the spirit with which they rode, and the generally fine breed of horses that paraded before the spectator, although a sporadic mule was running along here and there among them. These animals are generally tabooed

---

[1] Stuart's headquarters formed "a semicircle round one side of the beautiful little valley in which the pleasant village of Orange Court-house is situated. . . ," wrote Borcke (II, 258). See also Blackford, p. 206; *Mit Schwert und Feder*, pp. 110-112.

in the cavalry, as well as in the artillery, since they are gun shy.

In May we stayed in the wonderful district around Culpeper and were frequently visited by Mrs. Stuart, Mrs. W. H. Lee, and other ladies, who helped essentially in making the monotonous camp life pleasant with their genial conversation.[2]

There was a false alarm on June 6. Everything was made ready to march off. My baggage weighing more than fifty pounds was sent into the city, and the wagons were loaded. Not until the following day did the division advance, the headquarters of which were established in a pretty little forest near Brandy Station. In the meantime, General Lee had come up the Rappahannock from the camp at Fredericksburg, and he held an ostentatious review on June 8, evidently to see whether Hooker was following him.[3] We had still not seen anything of the enemy.

A courier suddenly rushed breathlessly into our tent at about 3:30 o'clock on the next morning and harshly jolted me out of my sleep with the cry: "Yankees in our headquarters!" whereupon I heard turmoil and firing near at hand. We pulled the astounded Borcke, my host, from the covers, and with a few leaps we were in Stuart's tent and in the open with him.[4] We saw immediately that greatest confusion prevailed on the very next hill, perhaps from 200 to 300 feet in front of us, where [Brig.] General [John M.] Jones, in command of the vanguard brigade, had his head-

---

[2] Borcke, II, 258-259, states that "provisions of every sort were abundant" at the camp. "The weather was perfect" and the region renowned "for the beauty of its women."

[3] *Ibid.*, II, 267: "Next day, [June 8] the cavalry corps had the honour of being reviewed by our Commander-in-chief [and] the whole of Hood's division, amounting to about 10,000 men, who were present as lookers-on, at their own request." Blackford, pp. 212-213, also describes the review, adding that it was the "last of our frolics for a long time, for on the morrow we were to begin the fighting which was kept up almost daily until two weeks after the battle of Gettysburg. . . ."

[4] Borcke states (*Die grosse Reiterschlacht* . . . , p. 148) that he aroused Scheibert, but Scheibert wrote (*Mit Schwert und Feder*, p. 116) that he "pulled von Borcke out of the covers," adding, "Strange to say, he was of the opinion that he had awakened me."

quarters. The demolishing of tents, the shouting, the firing, and the racing of loose horses showed how near the enemy was. Stuart's headquarters was on its feet in an instant, and the couriers were in the saddle, flying off in all directions with Stuart's short notes. Several squadrons of our regiments as well, alerted by fugitives and couriers and quickly in the saddle, were already appearing and were on the point of checking the first blow, with vigorous counterattacks, as always. All brigades were on the scene in hardly an hour, and Stuart was master of his entire division, then numbering 8,000 cavalrymen with about 20 guns of horse artillery, of which somewhat more than a third were rifled. With his characteristic energy, he ordered the mischief-makers attacked from all sides, and stability was soon achieved. After the enemy horsemen had withdrawn, the cavalry encountered seven infantry regiments drawn up parallel to a long fence protecting them from attack, who opened a relatively well-aimed fire. General Stuart now attempted to hold the infantry's front with sharpshooters (dismounted cavalrymen, all of whom are skilled marksmen) and with artillery, in order to overrun the flanks with W. Lee's brigade (son of the Commanding General). The latter made bold attempts to do this by trying to leap over a well-defended, low stone wall with his cavalry, but the efforts were in vain, despite great losses, and he himself, who ordered the same brigade into the attack three times, was severely wounded at the head of his men.

The fighting came to a stop, and General Stuart now sought by other means at least to paralyze the resistance of the infantry until General Lee, who was located about three miles to the rear, could arrive with infantry reinforcements.[5]

I had been watching the action for some time. The fighting was not spirited, and since I was disturbed about my diary, which I had left in the tent, I rode back from the front to the hill where our camp had stood.[6]

---

[5] Borcke, II, 268-272; Blackford, pp. 213-216.
[6] *Ibid.*, p. 121, states that on June 7 the camp had been "moved to 'Fleetwood,' an old plantation residence near Brandy Station."

I noticed with astonishment that the tents were struck, and that instead of them, cavalry now crowned the [Fleetwood] hill.[7] Although a quartermaster who was riding up said that these were our reserves, their great numbers still seemed suspicious to me, and we were soon informed about the true character of this marshaling of troops by several couriers who raced past at full speed and shouted, "Yankees in our rear!" At the same time, flying riders, whose general appearance caused me to suspect similar reports, seemed to rush up to Stuart from all sides. We had been surrounded by 10,000 men while seven regiments of infantry were holding too strongly the attention of our commander at the front. If the enemy had now launched a strong and boldly resolute attack on the astounded brigades, without letting the leaders come to their senses, and had vigorously exploited the surprise, there would probably have been nothing left for the startled troops to do but to fight their way out of the battle individually. But Stuart, who hurried to the top of a small hill where he could look around, had time to intervene. Two regiments of Jones's brigade were dispatched at once to the rear to cut an opening for the passage of the train, and the other brigades were ordered in the meantime to the center of the circle, whereby the sharpshooters were left facing the enemy to hold the infantry in the front line.

The two regiments that were ordered to break through to the rear were not as well disciplined as the other brigades, and, forgetting the proverb "Haste makes waste," they came up in a wild race, though in reasonably close order, and were naturally out of breath before the real impact came, so much the more so, since they had to hurry up a hill. The Northern cavalry received them (in a miserable way) with a salvo fired at a distance of a hundred paces, which, by way of exception, not only stopped the attack this time, but also

[7] Borcke, II, 276, says, "The greater part of our corps was now placed along the ridge . . . whilst further on, in the plains below, were arrayed in line of battle many thousand Federal cavalry, supported by two divisions of infantry, whose glittering bayonets could be easily discerned as they deployed from the distant woods."

drove the frightened horsemen back some distance. Again
the enemy cavalry had an opportunity to inflict great damage at this place, but it was satisfied to advance calmly,
while Major von Borcke rushed into the midst of the fleeing
soldiers, drew his large, straight sword, and called upon
them in a loud voice to resume the attack. But cavalry that
has once scattered and been beaten is hard to use in a real
attack on the same day. That also proved to be true here.
Hardly had they come upon the enemy when they again
turned around after receiving a salvo, and the Major was
not able to rally the men again properly by persuasion
either of words or of deeds.[8]

The instant that was momentarily highly critical for our
cavalry passed without misfortune only because of the
enemy's inactivity. In the turn of a hand, Stuart had in
the meantime issued orders to his forces, again proving himself to be an able cavalry general. He sent one brigade up
from the other side of the fateful hill headlong against the
lines that were then under attack, and ordered one and a
half brigades coming up in line to wheel a little and take
the direction toward the main body of the enemy. Thus he
opened up the opportunity for a fine attack in regimental
echelons, whereby, in a manner of speaking, wave after
wave roared against the frightened cavalry masses of the
Northerners. Fighting was soon general, and even the
Federals, who as a rule never attacked, made exceptions at
many places on this day by boldly using their sabers. The
artillery afforded the background for the wild spectacle,
which unfortunately soon became enveloped in a big cloud
of dust and smoke. The fighting spun out more and more
from all sides, moving on the entire periphery of a circle
with a diameter of about a thousand paces. Dust clouds
rolled rapidly toward the forest (signs of pursuit), and
many floated up, giving news of an unsuccessful attack.
Wherever the fighting faltered, Stuart sent squadrons into

---

[8] *Ibid.*, II, 278, states that Stuart ordered Borcke to lead the rally,
that his horse twice fell in the charge, and that under his leadership
the "gallant Virginians" broke the Federal line, driving the enemy in
disorderly flight. . . ."

the flanks or sent case shots thundering in. It is impossible to present the individual scenes of this twelve hour battle, particularly since a man could see and hear only what was happening right around and before him. Shrapnel, case shot, and pistol balls hissed through the air from all sides. Excited, riderless horses were running about like scalded cats, and Negroes in mortal terror ran from one side to the other with their masters' horses, not finding protection anywhere against enemy shells. Ambulances assembled in the center in a thick mass. Men who were running away toppled over one another without sense or reason. Lost soldiers asked about their regiments, and couriers sought Stuart out to request speedy reinforcement. In short, it was chaos, the like of which occurs only in cavalry engagements and which alone conveys a clear and vivid picture of war. Energetic activity, instantaneous resolution, calmness, cool reflection, and again reckless audacity were the intermittent fevers. The horse artillery behaved nobly beyond praise. It was cool, cold-blooded, and calm in aiming. Most of the artillerists sang merry songs in the midst of the fight, calmly took the sponge from the hands of comrades who had been shot, and continued loading while singing. (They were, moreover, the only ones in the army who always had brandy, and for whom there was much indulgence.)

The General had not a man to send against an enemy brigade coming out of the woods—he had already thrown all reserves into the tumult—and thus he ordered up two batteries, enjoining the men racing up at full speed to fire deliberately, for they had to stop the full thrust alone. It was successful. After the men had deliberately aimed and fired eight rounds of case shot, which exploded right before the heads of the horsemen, the enemy troops wheeled and entered the fight only after a quarter of an hour, when forces were again available for counterattack.[9]

We saw the circle open up gradually and the clouds of

[9] Freeman, III, 31-32, describes the Battle of Brandy Station (also called Fleetwood Hill) as "the greatest cavalry engagement of the entire war." See also Blackford, p. 215.

dust move farther and farther into the forest, where the fire of small arms also indicated the direction of the fight. Moreover, we could always tell by the yelling of the Confederates where success had been achieved.

After the enemy cavalry had again made a stand, it withdrew across the Rappahannock with the infantry regiments that protected it from pursuit, so that the battle had already been fought to a conclusion when General Lee arrived with help at about three o'clock in the afternoon.

The losses on both sides were not insignificant, even though the results were not great, and one could see by the wounds that in many sectors the saber had not been spared. It is strange that the American really does not know how to use the saber well, since he has never had occasion to use it in time of peace. Therefore, it frequently happened in pursuits at the beginning of the war with the Confederate, a natural, steady rider, would rather sheathe his saber, chase the Unionist, who was barely balancing himself on his horse, seize him by the collar from the rear, and pull him off without difficulty, capturing man and horse.

Two members of Stuart's staff fell on this day. A third was captured.[10]

I had reason on that evening to be happy for having come through safely, for in addition to the numerous shells of all types that zoomed past us, there once landed right before me a shrapnel shell, the many pieces of which buzzed past my ears, almost touching me, and at another time, when the General's staff was lying down among their horses right after the engagement, a shell fell in the middle of the circle, fortunately without exploding, but just scattering the group for a moment.

When it was all over, I rode after my diary, which I believed to be lost, and I learned to my great satisfaction at Brandy Station that our fine quartermaster, Major [Norman] Fitz Hugh [sic], with his characteristic cunning,

---

[10] *Ibid.*, p. 216, identifies the killed as Lieut.-Col. Frank Hampton and Col. Sol Williams and the captured as Lieut. Robert H. Goldsborough. See *ORA*, 1 series, XXVII, pt. 2, 684-685.

had taken our baggage and Stuart's important papers through the enemy lines to safety in the woods. The enemy had just had time in our depots to pour the grain out in the woods, so that we who rode along that way let our hungry horses eat their fill, while I myself lay down under a tree, completely exhausted by strain and by the sickness from which I had hardly recovered.[11]

From my position I saw the expected infantry columns moving up. In the lead, to my great delight, was General Lee with his staff, to whom I was able immediately to give authentic news about the fight, which pleased the old gentleman all the more, since the men who had fled in the morning, the officials coming from Brandy Station, etc., had naturally given a very gloomy picture of the engagement. He was kind enough to invite me to his headquarters for the approaching campaign, and I accepted with profound gratitude. Again we rode forward, examined the enemy position on the front, visited the hospital, and then rode to headquarters at Culpeper, where Stuart had previously had his camp. The enemy had pulled back across the Rappahannock in our presence.

[11] Borcke, II, 280-281. As the men rode back towards "our old headquarters," Borcke saw the battlefield "thickly strewn with carcasses, on which hundreds of turkey buzzards had been gorging themselves. . . ."

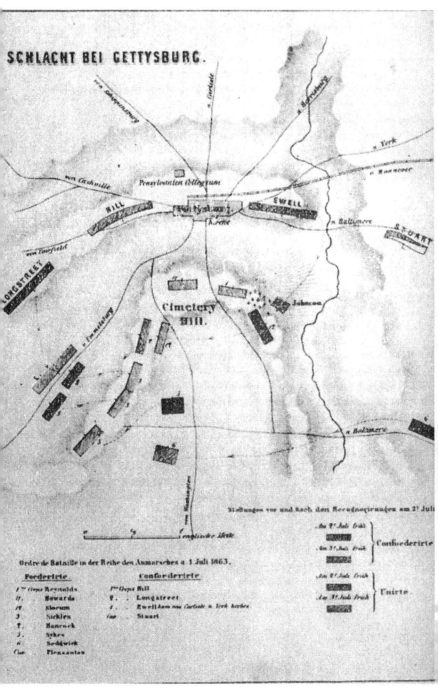

Battle of Gettysburg

Chapter V

Invasion of Pennsylvania, Battle of Gettysburg, and Retreat

In spite of the approaching storm, all was quiet and peaceful at headquarters, as my diary says, for the General spread cheer and good feeling round about like the sun that refreshes the plants. Thus, these days in the freshly fragrant woods are to be numbered among the best of my life. I used the period of leisure to augment my sketches of Chancellorsville with copies of rather large maps and to increase my information about the army, the people, and politics through conversations, especially with Major Venable, who again shared his time with me.

Major Venable was a genuinely representative Southerner, unselfish and pure of heart, and a sacrificing patriot whose character aroused my genuine respect. I hope that I may some day be in position to repay his devoted friendship.[1]

General Stuart, who reported to the Commanding General on the Battle of Brandy Station during this period, was kind enough to bring along my greatly missed diary.

Here in this camp was now spun the thread of one of the greatest invasive marches, only slightly suspected in the army and directed solely by the hands of the President, of General Lee, and of the three corps commanders.

---

[1] See above, Chapter II, n. 2. After the war, when Col. Venable visited Scheibert in Silesia and Borcke in Prussia, the latter flew a Prussian flag and a Confederate flag from atop his castle (Blackford, pp. 220-221).

Before I continue the story, it will be necessary to let the military reader take another look at General Lee's strategy in order to lead him through the labyrinth of movements.

It is clear that the uninterrupted *pursuit of the enemy* definitely required by our modern theory would have been an absurdity after the Battle of Chancellorsville. For if General Lee, with the remainder of his army, now numbering hardly 40,000 men, had succeeded in crossing the Rappahannock in the face of the enemy of three times his own strength, and in forcing him from one strong position to another, without suffering *even one defeat* that might have jeopardized the entire existence of the South, then he would have been able to press forward to the fortified city of Washington and would thus have come into possession of a region completely drained by war, which he would have had to abandon again as soon as possible in order to get closer to Richmond, the base of his supplies and operations.

Therefore, he preferred to reorganize his army with ready recruits, while a reduction, at least in men with a record of service, was in prospect in the North because of the termination of periods of enlistment, and he replenished his greatly depleted military supplies and his almost exhausted artillery munitions for a greater objective, a large scale invasion of the Northern States.[2]

Several reasons impelled the President and General Lee to this campaign, particularly the great shortage of food supplies that had already led to the men's receiving half rations. This deficiency could be relieved considerably by marching into fruitful Pennsylvania. Futhermore, there was hope, by means of a strong offensive thrust, of giving superiority to the Democratic Party in the North, which, like a great part of the people, was dissatisfied with the government's currently foolish manner of conducting the war. Thirdly, there was, as a result of the adverse or indecisive results at Vicksburg and in Tennessee, a desire to find a slogan to arouse the impatient populace to new endeavors, and finally, to force favorable terms of peace in

2 See Freeman, III, 12ff.

the event of a great, brillant success in the heart of the country, in the rich ports of the North or in Washington.

From this one realizes the high stakes involved in the game and understands how it happened that a feverish tension must have prevailed from the General down to the youngest private soldier on this expedition.

On the other hand, the risks of an invasion of the North, considered from all sides, were not small. Especially was the government stripping its country of almost all troops, so that with the enemy's superiority, a detached and sufficiently strong corps, led by a bold general, could easily force its way to Richmond while a major army was holding General Lee in check. Furthermore, the Southern army, completely detached from its base and able to carry only a limited amount of munitions, might well be cut off and completely destroyed. Indeed, the offshoot of *every* battle that did not end in *absolute* victory had to be calamitous for the existence of the invading army if the enemy general had a little more than ordinary enterprising spirit. But the world belongs to the courageous.

After Lee had seen that Hooker was following him and did not have the courage to advance immediately and directly on Richmond after the position at Fredericksburg had been abandoned, he ordered the advance as follows:

The First Corps ([Gen.] A. P. Hill), as a rear guard, consisting of the divisions of Anderson, Pender, and Heth, held Hooker on the Rappahannock with continuous harassment, etc., at the same time indirectly covering the passes across the Allegheny Mountains.

The Second Corps ([Lt.-Gen. R. S.] Ewell), as advance guard, with the divisions of [Maj.-Gen. Edward] Johnson (Stonewall), Early, and Rodes, left Culpeper on the 10th, entered Winchester with its leading elements on the evening of the 13th, which place Ewell captured on the 14th, and then moved unimpeded on forced marches across the Potomac to Maryland and into Pennsylvania, where it spread such terror and panic that all the militia was called out.

(It marched in three days from Culpeper to Winchester,

70 miles, that is, more than five German miles a day, on bad roads across the mountain range.)

The Third Corps ([Lt.-Gen. James] Longstreet), as the main body, with McLaws', [Maj.-Gen. George E.] Pickett's and Hood's divisions, started moving on the 15th, held the center between the two previously mentioned corps to help wherever the cavalry, which covered the passes and the right flank, was not able to fulfill its assignment, and finally, to prevent Hill's being cut off or any interruption of the long, extended line of march.

The Cavalry (Stuart), in addition to the task previously indicated, had the order to cover the movements of the main army by defending the passes of the Blue Ridge Mountains to the east, while the army was marching to the west of these heights, between them and the Allegheny Mountains (along the Valley of Virginia).

Our staff made the march with the main body of troops.[3] On the way, two days after the Battle of Winchester, I rode into this city to get an explanation of its remarkable capture, and I found a lively, happy spirit there.   The inhabitants were glad that they could at last breathe freely after long oppression by the notorious enemy general, [R. A.] Milroy, who was later brought before a court-martial. The soldiers had obtained an almost complete supply of new clothes with the abundant booty and had outfitted themselves with articles of equipment, waterproof cloths, etc. I also received from the commanding officer a new, beautiful water canteen (tin flask with a cloth cover) as a gift to commemorate the fight.   General Lee, to whom the supplies were offered so that he might have first choice, smilingly accepted a large Chester cheese, which was often quite appetizing to us in the following weeks.[4]

---

[3] Scheibert remained with Lee's staff throughout the Gettysburg campaign, as will be seen, and Borcke, of course, rode with Stuart. On June 19 Borcke was severely wounded in a cavalry skirmish near Aldie (Blackford, pp. 218-219; Borcke, II, 293-296).

[4] Ewell had captured Winchester on June 15-16, taking 4,000 prisoners and opening the roads northward to the Potomac River (Freeman, III, 38).

Even the numerous captured and wounded enemy soldiers seemed to be quite content. The Confederate soldier really treated his prisoners decently, and even in Richmond the inhabitants neither rejoiced nor reviled when prisoners marched in, since that was considered to be tactless; instead, they would then calmly and seriously restrain themselves.

So far as I have seen prisoners and prisons, I can only say that I have observed no torture or bad treatment of any sort, nor have I heard complaints. In times when even the army was put on half rations, indeed, on quarter rations of bacon and corn, when no vegetables, butter, or other trimmings were to be had, it was in the nature of circumstances that the food seemed highly deficient and poor, especially to the previously abundantly provisioned Northerners. It is possible that one or another warden abused his office here and there in isolated prisons in this time of unrest and trouble, but I as a credible witness (I hope) can say with assurance, as can the foreign gentlemen from Europe who were over there with me, that any bad treatment of prisoners was not only *not in the nature of principle,* but that the noble spirit of the humane General Lee, as well as the humane mind of the abused President Jefferson Davis, vouch for the fact that the captured enemy was treated as well as circumstances permitted.

Let the *whole, stern truth* be brought to light, so that at least posterity may some day judge *correctly* as to where there was sin, for only one who is ignorant of American justice can consider the now partly completed legal proceedings against Davis, Lee, Wirtz, etc.,[5] to be anything but a perversion of the law before public opinion.

Moreover, here comes to light again the characteristic observation that the most fantastic rumors about the hostile treatment of prisoners circulate wherever war is being waged.

General Lee was received with respectful honor by the

---

[5] In 1868, when Scheibert's book was printed, Capt. Henry Wirtz, of Andersonville fame, had been dead three years—executed by Federal authorities on Nov. 10, 1865 (see Miller, ed., VII, 176-180).

inhabitants, to whom he had given the opportunity to return from the mountain gorges and visit their farms again, or from whom he had removed the heavy yoke of hostile spite by his entry, and many an old matron by the side of the road bestowed with trembling hands her blessings upon the old and modest gentleman. He would accept no other gifts from the hands of his admirers, with the possible exception of occasional refreshments, and he refused to accept meals and lodging. He always slept in the open or in a half-tent, and he was satisfied with plain camp food, which was taken in the morning even before daybreak, so that we might be in the saddle at four o'clock sharp.

High spirits naturally prevailed at headquarters. The success at Winchester seemed to be an auspicious sign for the approaching campaign, and the panic of the North, which was openly expressed in the Unionist press, also did much to enliven the spirit. The less opportunity the press in the South had to discuss the plans of the leaders, since General Lee tolerated no writers at headquarters,[6] the better were we at headquarters informed by the new Northern newspapers brought through by the scouts every day, not only about the anxious excitement of the Northern States, but we were also always informed in advance about enemy marches and the embarrassed feeling in Hooker's council, who had "lost" the enemy.

In addition to the lively mood, which we foreigners naturally strongly shared, there was evident in the Southern army a special trait of character that I must not withhold. Although (in frequent speculation) brilliant results were prophesied for this expedition in case of success, still, we were always hearing the words: "We just want to win our freedom; just let them recognize our states rights and our independence," this despite the fact that we were always marching through a waste of enemy devastation and plunder. *"We will not avenge ourselves.* Vengeance belongs to heaven alone!"

---

[6] Scheibert undoubtedly means domestic writers, because he soon introduces "Mr. Lawley, the correspondent of the London *Times*, who went on all expeditions. . . ." See Freeman, III, 464; IV, 159.

Only a major of Longstreet's staff contradicted this opinion by saying (in agreement with a part of the press) that the enemy had to be shown what war was, what it meant to suffer injustice—only then would he yield and abate! This utterance was earnestly rejected by all and was found to be so contradictory to the somewhat solemn spirit prevalent, at least on the staffs, that many men avoided association with the gentleman.

I call as witnesses of my assertion those neutral Europeans who stayed at the headquarters of the Army of Northern Virginia, most of whom have already literally confirmed my statements in articles, etc. Such confirmation seems to be all the more necessary in Germany, since there prevails here an unspeakably distorted opinion of American affairs, inasmuch as only the German-American newspapers are considered as authorities, most of which are very poorly edited, and which try to make up for lack of expert knowledge with exciting products of fantasy, and for want of logic, with provocative tirades bordering on the ridiculous. Since the gentlemen will be our companions in the following campaigns, I hereby introduce them to the reader; Mr. [Francis C.] Lawley, the correspondent of the London *Times,* who went on all expeditions in spite of his sickliness, and who was highly esteemed by all of his acquaintances as a gentleman and amiable man;[7] he was the successor to the well-known William Russell, with whose sharp, biting pen of bubbling wit he could not compete, but whom he excelled in tactful, restrained demeanor and in a calm view of things, so that he whetted the appetite of the reader less, to be sure, but did more to promote a true understanding of the facts. His reports were at that time the best that appeared in Europe concerning American affairs.

Colonel Fremantle of the English Coldstream Guards, who had landed in Mexico and had made the trip on horseback from there through the Southern States, also came upon the

---

[7] See Introduction, p. 10. Lawley's sixty essays appeared in the *Times,* Oct. 7, 1862-Apr. 29, 1865. Fremantle met Scheibert on June 22 at Lee's headquarters.

army in the Valley of Virginia. Upon his return to England, he made his name prominent in English military literature with vivid sketches of his sojourn with the Confederate Army. This gentleman was also able to win the hearts of everyone with his open, candid behavior. Captain Fitzgerald Ross of the Austrian hussars, who had secretly slipped from Baltimore across the Potomac to the Southern States, also reached our army somewhat later. I became associated with him on friendly terms not only as a fellow countryman, but also because we were later billeted together, and because we shared our joys and sorrows during the siege of Charleston.[8]

All three of these gentlemen found a friendly reception at General Longstreet's headquarters. I emphasize so much the more the prevalent spirit of the army, which we shall later see in action, especially since the South has at its disposal no means of defending, even in an appreciable measure, its name, which is spitefully besmirched by slander.

We have established the position of the main army at this time on the may [p. 95], but we have mentioned only casually the cavalry, which, under Stuart's prudent leadership, had to fight hard and bloody battles at the passes of the Blue Ridge summits, which snatched many a fine cavalryman from the ranks without its becoming possible to win laurels against the great, superior force of the enemy.

The reason for entrusting to the cavalry these sections of the country, which can really be best defended with infantry, lies in the fact that General Lee did not want to dissipate his corps or show the enemy how important the covering of his flank was, since the presence of Stuart's cavalry, which was to be found everywhere and nowhere, gave the enemy no indication that the main army was also to be found there.

Soon fortune also led me into these passes, whereby I also got a look at the mode of combat in that region. Indeed, I

[8] See below, pp. 140ff. After meeting Lee, Longstreet, Hill, Scheibert and others at Lee's headquarters, Ross was accompanied back to Chambersburg by Scheibert, who helped him get a room at the Franklin Hotel. Lawley was there also, ill in bed. See Fremantle, p. 123.

received news one morning that Major von Borcke had been severely wounded in the engagement at Aldie, and that he longed to talk to me. With some concern, I saddled my white horse immediately and rode as quickly as possible, in view of the great distance, by way of Berryville and Millwood to the flooded Shenandoah, the ford of which I tried to follow by memory, which I succeeded in doing, with the exception of a few stretches, by keeping upstream and thus always coming back to the ford as soon as I could no longer touch the bottom. I passed over the frequently mentioned mountain range by way of Paris, and in the little town of Upperville, where a fight was then in full swing, I found Borcke lying pale and weak in bed in the house of Dr. [Talcott] Eliason (of Stuart's staff), just able to whisper a few words. The ball had gone through his neck and had wounded his windpipe. Nevertheless, he was forced to ride two miles after the wounding in order to get away from the battle. While I was still standing by his bed, a messenger came from Stuart with greetings for me and with the order to carry my wounded fellow countryman to Paris immediately, since the General was defending the last position only for Borcke's sake and would then be forced to take up a position in the pass itself to evade the superior enemy force. But since the patient and the doctor both firmly declared that moving such a distance, for which Stuart had made his own ambulance available, was impossible in view of the condition of the wound, and since von Borcke firmly stated that he would not be captured alive, mindful of the fact that the Unionists dragged every important officer off to Washington as a trophy, regardless of his wounds, there remained nothing to do in this emergency but either to hide him in the woods aside from the position or, if possible, to conceal him in the home of one of the patriotic gentlemen living in those woods.[9]

[9] Borcke, II, 293-302: "The battle seemed raging in the immediate vicinity, and the shells bursting right over the village, when, to my great joy, my Prussian friend Captain Scheibert entered my room. At the first news of my misfortune, he had hastened from the distant headquarters of our army, bringing along with him General Longstreet's private ambulance. . . ." See also Blackford, pp. 219-220.

Therefore, we loaded him carefully on the ambulance and drove slowly along the stony mountain, since the poor wounded man winced with every little jolt. We could tell by the noise that the battle was coming nearer and nearer. Our men were already withdrawing from the forest, riding westward into the hills, and we now found ourselves with our beloved burden *between* the two fighting parties, apparently driving along calmly. The excitement, the reason for which we withheld from Borcke, increased from minute to minute, for several enemy cavalrymen could already be seen, and riderless and bloody horses, among them a white one with blood-red head, were running around by the road as a sign of recent combat. We caught four of them and took them along with us. We were about to hide our friend in the foliage and get away, when we fortunately came upon soft ground near a hospitable house, and now we hurried to it with our wagon as fast as we could. Von Borcke was quickly removed and carried to the porch, and the unknown master of the house was briefly informed about the cause of the surprise. The latter urged us to flee in all haste, while von Borcke first peremptorily demanded and then fervently begged us to take him along, which would have meant his death, but we scurried off posthaste through the woods and across streams and fences. It was due only to the agile jumping of the horses and to the ready following of the seized mounts that we escaped from the pursuing cavalrymen without loss. Everything seemed quiet after a half hour, and we all met again by way of circuitous roads in Paris, where Stuart, with a sad look, inquired about his friend.

He was disconsolate when he heard that his chief of staff was probably in enemy hands, and he was not appeased until he was convinced by our story in detail that everything humanly possible had been done for Borcke. "I must dig him out again," he said. "He may still be lying there unobserved!" This idea of digging him out was also shared by all cavalrymen in the group, whose eyes beamed with every reference to the major, whom they always called "our gallant von Borcke."

I remained in Paris for some time to arrange a few things for Borcke and to inform myself about what would be done in his interest. Since I soon saw that his case was in the best hands in the world, I sent Henry [Borcke's Negro servant] ahead to Millwood with the Major's horses and with my own exhausted mount, and I started on the way late on one of von Borcke's horses, in deep worry about the fate of my fellow countryman. When I came to the top of the pass, I saw the brave General Longstreet coming up at the head of a brigade. He asked me immediately why I looked so worried, contrary to my usual appearance. I told him briefly the reason for my sorrow, which he heard with close attention. Thereupon he said to me, "Here you have my hand as a pledge that your friend will be rescued early in the morning if he is still in the house you mentioned and is not carried away. It would be a shame for the army to leave such a brave officer in the hands of the enemy when it is still possible to rescue him." The brigadier general who was riding along beside him expressed himself in a similarly friendly manner by adding that he was happy to be the very man who would receive the order to liberate the universal favorite. Thus I rode on, naturally with a relieved heart, since I knew that I no longer had anything to worry about. My foresight was well-founded, for I later received by courier from General Stuart the news that von Borcke had been fortunately rescued, that he was on the way to Richmond, and that his wound gave hopes of healing. The affair had taken the following course: Despite von Borcke's reluctance and anger, he was carried to a back room as soon as we had left him and was locked up by the previously mentioned gentleman and his servants, which was done at the very moment when the enemy cavalry was already at the door asking about the officer who had just alighted. The gentleman pointed to us as we were just disappearing in the woods and thus put the pursuers on the wrong track. He then treated the soldiers with refreshments to the best of his ability, until they were informed of the approach of a rather large body of troops, whereupon they quit the district of their own accord, leaving von Borcke in the arms of happy friends. Von Borcke told me later that, despite his anger over his miserable condition and our disappearing with his horses, he still had to laugh out loud at the scene that played between me and Henry: The other gentlemen had ridden on into the woods, leading their extra horses, when Henry, completely unaware of the whole situation, believed that he could not leave unused the pretty meadow lying next to the woods, and before I knew what was happening, he unbridled the horses to let them graze with the white mules, while I could already hear the shouts of the Yankees behind us. Since he did not understand my English, and as the critical moment permitted no extensive explanation, I spoke to him in German, and by slapping him, shaking him, and striking him with the flat of my saber, I first got him on the white Katy, and then with long flourishes of my saber I scared the latter into the woods at a gallop, where we probably disappeared like amusing caricatures. I did not consider Henry to be reliable after this scene, but here as later he showed himself to be good, though very dumb.

I tried to get back to headquarters as soon as possible, and thus I rode on the same evening to the Shenandoah River, which, however, I found to be so swollen that I did not dare ford it in the dark, and while my horse was grazing, I camped in the bitter cold night on a damp meadow under a pair of old, tattered trousers that had been picked up by Henry on the battlefield. About midnight, when I could no longer endure the cold, I crawled into a flour sack that had been lent to me, in which I slept splendidly until morning, with my head lying in my saddle. Then I rode to General Lee's headquarters, which I found in Berryville.

The head of our snake was now in Hagerstown, the body was in the Valley of Virginia, and the tail was on the way to the passes of the Blue Ridge Mountains. The marches of the troops evoked my genuine admiration. The order of march was exemplary, with an average accomplishment of eighteen to twenty-three miles daily by each corps without a day of respite, with sections marching in close order, and only a few lay exhausted by the side of the road, despite the great heat. The tempo of the march was very moderate, with ninety to a hundred paces a minute.

Now the marching columns kept regular distances, whereby the advance guard of General Ewell was penetrating deep in the direction of Pennsylvania when we with the center along the magnificently beautiful Valley of Virginia were arriving at Williamsport on the Potomac, which we crossed at a very rocky ford. Thus we entered Maryland after we had supervised the construction of a pontoon bridge at Falling Water, the completion of which took two full days with the use of less than twenty men. Headquarters went by way of Hagerstown and State Line into Pennsylvania, the first decidely hostile state, where we pitched our tents in the rain.[10]

On the 27th we entered Chambersburg, the first enemy city of considerable size, which also clearly disclosed its sentiment. The city had everything to fear, for the news had come shortly before our entrance that the cities of Richmond, Louisiana [sic] and Darien, Georgia, had been put to the torch by the Northerners out of sheer rapacity. One can imagine how this treatment enraged the feelings of the men. Indeed, even the General, who as he said, had spent many lovely days in the "little jewel box" of Darien, was deeply grieved by the destruction of this city.

In reply, the "Chief of the Rebels," the leader of the "bloodhounds," etc., issued Order No. 73, which is in my possession in the original. . . .[11]

* * * * * * * * * * * * *

I was struck upon our entrance by an attraction that showed the good nature of the common soldiers. An extremely tactless woman held before herself her five year old boy, who was waving the enemy flag, which was naturally especially odious in a civil war. I stopped to see the effect

---

[10] See Freeman, III, 18ff.
[11] Lee's famous Order No. 73, as quoted by Scheibert (omitted here), may be seen in *ORA*, 1 series, XXVII, pt. 3, 942-943.

of this provocation. But troop after troop marched past either with cheers for the "charming old flag" or with groans for the old Yankee rag, or some other unpleasant witticism, without even one's having reproved in bitter words the impropriety which even I as a neutral felt.

The excellent rum and cognac in Chambersburg were poured into the streets after the doctors had replenished their stocks, since the entire *army had voluntarily abjured spiritous alcohol,* although there was no substitute for this drink except water and a decoction of parched corn or acorns, or sassafras tea.

Payment was made for everything in Chambersburg, and not a single excess occurred, despite the amazing impudence of the merchants, so that Captain Ross, who had been in Solferino, said to me with surprise one day: "Here the enemy is really being handled with kid gloves!"

The General set up his headquarters at Chambersburg in *tents adjacent to the town. Nobody was quartered in the city proper, because Southern laws did not permit the quartering of troops in private homes, even in their own country. Nor was anybody admitted into the town, which was occupied by sentries, without authorization by a pass from General Lee himself,* so that no friction could occur. The General himself questioned all, especially women, as to whether they had any complaints against his troops, telling them that they should not hesitate to specify the regiment and that he would exact strictest punishment for such trespasses.

The army as such was not only not indignant over these disciplinary measures and Order No. 73, but was even proud of them, although a great part of it had arrived with vengeful feelings. I heard many private soldiers with whom I discussed it say: "Indeed, this noble order is worthy of our cause, and we gladly obey it. It is just abominable that these Yankees don't even feel how well we behave toward them!"

In general, the press and the people at home did not understand the great and noble purposes of the President and of our commanders, who acted in accord in this respect, but instead, they preached retribution, vengeance, and devastation.

But the press had no power, although every common soldier read the newspapers every day, which were available at ridiculously low prices.

We broke camp early on July 1 and went to Cashtown. The road was full of wagons and troops, since the corps were marching in close order, for A. P. Hill had come up, and it was not easy to pass. We had hardly dismounted when cannon shots became audible at the front, and the frequently expected dispatch came, stating that *the enemy had attacked the head of our column*. These were the first harbingers of the bloody battles at *Gettysburg*, for the clash had occurred at the city by that name, and now the objective of the movements had finally been reached. We rode hurriedly to that place and arrived just at the right time to see the attack against a wooded hill which was near the city, and which was occupied by enemy infantry and numerous artillery units. Our men advanced in line as always. By way of exception, the Northerners launched a counterattack this time with a column, but it was fired upon from all sides and was besieged and forced back, and the Southerners would have entered the woods almost simultaneously with the Yankees if a flanking artillery position and a previously unobserved railroad cut had not held up the advance. But both sides rallied quickly, the Confederates down in the valley, and the Northerners in the woods, and with a new disposition, whereby the flanking battery was also attacked, the second assault of the Southern troops was successful, and the forest and the city were stormed with a shrill yell. The frightened enemy retired to a height known as Cemetery Hill. It was the I and the II Corps that effected a lodgment there. They lost 6,000 prisoners alone in the process, mostly Germans, again of the II Corps, along with the commanding general, [John F.] Reynolds.[12]

---

[12] Freeman, III, 71. In capturing the town of Gettysburg, the Confederates took "nearly 5000 bewildered prisoners [and] almost as

On the one hand, night brought the engagement to a stop, and on the other, the fact that General Lee had a long, extended column on the march, with only two divisions at his disposal, while he had to assume that he was confronted with the entire enemy force, the seven corps of Chancellorsville. Moreover, an unsuccessful engagement might cause him very great difficulty in the unfavorable position far from his base of operations. If General Lee had had any idea of the demoralized condition of the enemy, a continuation of the pursuit would surely have been ordered. This would have been even more successful with our advance guard's gaining control of Cemetery Hill, which was later to become so destructive for us.

The hill, which curved away from the city eccentrically in the shape of a horse shoe and was crowned by several patches of woods about 800 paces in diameter, was reconnoitered at dawn on July 2, after Ewell's corps had come up. General Lee made probing movements everywhere and hoped to maneuver the supposedly weaker Northerners out of position by drawing out the extreme flanks. For this reason, there were attacks on these points, which had no lasting success, since they had no concentration as a result of the spreading of the attacking troops and were also incoherent. Despite the display of extraordinary bravery, these very bloody battles had no decisive results. The positions of the various corps can be seen on the map. Since we did not gain mastery of the battlefield, I copied this map from the splendid works of Captain Chesney, the Englishman.[13]

I had ridden along the entire front on this day and had seen that even a moderately favorable view of the foreground was not to be had from any point in the valley, when I saw an oak tree on the mountain where General Lee was accustomed to stop, and in the tree Colonel Fremantle, whom I joined. From here the battlefield lay before us like

many dead and wounded lay on the ground. . . . The campaign of invasion could not have had a more auspicious opening."
[13] See Chesney, II, 50.

a panorama. On July 2 and 3, therefore, I did not move a step from the tree, from where I frequently had to report what I saw. My white horse was grazing in the grass below.[14]

General Lee was very much concerned and restless about General Stuart, of whom he had heard and seen nothing for several days, and whom he could have used well on this and the preceding day. News finally came in the evening that this bold general had marched across the Potomac at Seneca, between Washington and the enemy army, from which he took 200 wagons, and was now at York, from whence he was ordered up, and he rode ninety miles with 3,000 men without dismounting or feeding.

Lee would have preferred to have him present on July 1, *without* this daring venture, in order better to harvest the fruits of the victory of the first day, and he would also have preferred to have him fresh and able to fight, while the cavalry naturally required twenty-four hours of rest in order to be ready again for effective service after the long march.[15]

The enemy position, which was really formidable, was to be taken by storm on the next morning, and McLaws' and Pickett's divisions and two brigades of Anderson's division (of Longstreet's corps) were ordered to do this, so that our right flank was to bring the decision. Altogether, 15,000 men were designated for the attack. The enemy was probably still numerically superior to us, despite his losses of July 1.

A cannonade was to precede the attack in order to soften up the defenders, who were heavily concentrated on the hill. Therefore, an artillery battle between about 110 Confederate

---

[14] Fremantle, pp. 129-130, states that at five o'clock in the morning [July 2] he "climbed up a tree in company with Captain Schreibert [*sic*] of the Prussian army. Just below us were seated Generals Lee, Hill, Longstreet, and Hood, in consultation. . . ." On July 3 the two foreigners were joined by Lawley, who amused the others with his *un*-military questions. See Freeman, III, 90; Lonn, p. 362, and Introduction, p. 11.

[15] See Blackford, pp. 221-228, for a description of Stuart's whereabouts during these few days prior to July 2, and Freeman, III, 105, for his eventual arrival at Gettysburg.

and 80 Federal guns began at five o'clock in the morning and was carried on without interruption until four o'clock in the afternoon.

I could see from my perch the effect of every single shot. The cannons were 1200 to 2000 paces from one another, according to the various positions, and they fired mostly tempered, high-explosive shells and shrapnel, rarely percussion shells. The damage caused by the apparently frightful eleven hour cannonade, which was accompanied by scarcely any musket fire, is hardly worth mentioning. The shells were quite ineffective against our men, who were somewhat dispersed, while the Northern papers reported that their troops suffered severely on the closely and heavily manned hills. Thus the effect of this cannonade was as a whole insignificant, and the firing *was a very costly waste of powder* for the Confederates, who had moved far from their base—who had indeed detached themselves from it.

Not until 4:30 o'clock in the afternoon did General Lee order General Longstreet to attack. The latter was restrained with difficulty from taking the lead himself, and consequently, he directed the assault from the edge of the woods in the rear.[16] Pickett's division was made vanguard and formed the first line of battle with [Maj.-Gen. W. D.] Pender's, [Brig.-Gen. Robert] Garnett's and [Brig.-Gen. L. A.] Armistead's brigades, and the second with the brigades of [Brig.-Gen. J. J.] Pettigrew and [Maj-Gen. Cadmus M.] Wilcox. Both groups advanced in lines, with sharpshooters in the lead.

All of the troops were veterans, with the exception of Pettigrew's North Carolinians, who had only been in noncombatant service in their home state and were, therefore, not equal to the fearful task confronting them, which required a tenacity thoroughly tempered by fire. The brigades advanced with resolute bravery, but Pettigrew's left flank

---

[16] Scheibert tactfully omits mention of Lee's grave concern over Longstreet's delay in attacking the enemy (see *ibid.*, III, 90-106). However, in *Der Bürgerkrieg* . . . Scheibert makes it clear that at Gettysburg Lee was "care-worn" and his usual "quiet self-possessed calmness was wanting" (*SHSP*, V, 90, Jan.-Feb., 1877).

was to some extent "in the air." In spite of the fire that belched forth from forty throats against the brave men, the troops moved courageously up the hill and stormed calmly through the hail of shells. The foremost men actually reached the crest, jumped over the breastworks, planted their blue [sic] flags between the cannons, and seemed indeed to be masters of the important position. But the victory lasted only a few anxiously tense moments that were fraught with decision. The attack began to waver, and the unanchored wing was outflanked by a clever, enfilading maneuver of the enemy. Pettigrew's young troops, in a difficult position, to be sure, gave ground after courageous resistance and now also pulled the rear lines of the flank down the hill. The Southerners had no success in the center either. Instead of pushing forward, the leading brigades, which had lost all of their leaders (all staff officers), engaged in salvos that were exchanged with the enemy at distances of from thirty to a hundred paces, and they fought thereby at a decided disadvantage. The defenders, who were in consternation in the first moment, took courage when they noticed a pause, and they naturally soon brought a three-fold superiority in firearms to bear in the fight, arms which could not miss their targets. The impulse was broken by this. The lines were mowed down, and the brave men were laid low by the thousands. The failure of the left flank completely staggered the strength of the attack, and the bloody remnants of the Confederates now reluctantly fell back to take refuge from the terrible fire in the woods at the foot of the hill. But not all of them, for many fearless hearts who would not immediately leave the conquered posts remained among the cannons and were killed or captured.

Thus ended a scene, on the outcome of which America's future might depend.[17]

.   .   .   .

The army lost *three divisional commanders: Pender*

---

[17] Scheibert quotes a passage (omitted here) from Chesney, II, 91-92, in which he praises the valor of Pickett's troops, adding "these statements agree literally with mine."

(dead), Hood, and [Maj.-Gen. Harry] Heth (wounded), and twelve brigadier generals.

The battle, which I had been able to follow precisely, had hardly been over for a quarter of an hour when the edge of the woods on Cemetery Hill came to life and two brigades of Northerners sailed (pardon the unmilitary expression) down the slope in order to have the honor of the offensive just one time. But hardly had they come within fifty feet of the lower edge on the side occupied by the Southerners, in which plucky sharpshooters had established themselves, when they received a strong, well-aimed salvo and returned in wild retreat to the protecting height.

General Lee appeared in full grandeur, despite the unsuccessful attack. He was now as calm as usual, and he consoled in his solid and affable manner those who were coming despondently down the hill.

Here I shall let the Englishman, Colonel Fremantle, speak, who is also a witness for my statements. He writes of his sojourn in the South in a publication that is worth reading.[18]

.   .   .   .

I must mention in this connection the fact that the Confederates spoke very favorably of the conduct of the Union officers, who led their men in this battle with good and encouraging examples.

The memorable day closed with a cavalry attack. [Maj-Gen.] Kilpatrick, who believed that he would reap a bountiful harvest in the demoralized state of the Southerners, sent forward under [Brig.-Gen. A.] Farnsworth a brigade, which charged with great valor in an attack on our extreme right flank. Unfortunately, it was the Texans of Hood's division, distinguished for their steadfastness, against whom the blow was directed. Although the cavalry rode unharmed through the sharpshooters, it still came to destruction, for it was subjected to such a deliberate and well-aimed fire by the line, and by the sharpshooters who faced about, that only eighteen horsemen are said to have escaped, while it was

[18] Scheibert's quotations (omitted here) may be seen in Fremantle, pp. 135-136, 138.

rumored that Farnsworth, severely wounded, shot himself when he was about to be captured, a deed which marked him as a hero in the eyes of the army.

If we consider the end results, nothing *substantive* was either won or lost on this day; 15,000 men, two and a half divisions, to be sure, had made a vain, though bloody attack, with heavy losses, but the other six and a half divisions were completely intact, so that there was lengthy deliberation as to whether they should advance, retire, or stand. The circumstances, therefore, were not as critical as represented by my English companion, who drew conclusions about the totality of things too much on the basis of the mood and condition of a part of them. But the tremendous expenditure of munitions was determinative in the decision to retreat. General R. E. Lee had less than 100 rounds per cannon and thus was no longer in position to fight a battle lasting several days. He had to return to his base of operations, and this was the Rappahannock.

If we are to consider critically the General's plan, which is naturally an easy task after the fact, then let us first sketch at this point the General's purpose as he openly stated it, even after the battle, although he did not usually talk very much.

The purpose was to bring to the country a sense of the burden of war, to obtain provisions, and, if everything was successful, circumstances permitting, to hold the entire North in check, and perhaps to win the independence of the country with this single expedition.

For this purpose the march was ordered in a long line covered by the Blue Ridge Mountains, in the course of which, as I have already explained, the army was extended like a snake in order to hold the enemy in the *rear* and to push forward forcefully at the *front*, while one corps and the cavalry secured the center and maintained continuity. The army gave up its base behind the Potomac, hastily assembling in a concentric mass. [Gen. George G.] Meade always remained on the line between the army and Washington and finally encountered General Lee at Gettysburg. If

the latter should succeed in beating and shocking the Northern army so sharply that he could hold it in check with a
small force, then the entire North would stand open to him
without the slightest defense, except the scorned militia, and
he would be able to enter unhindered the seaports from
Baltimore and Philadelphia up to Boston and New York,
which would be tantamount to dictating peace to the North.

But General Lee believed that the destruction of the
enemy army could be brought about only by placing the
main emphasis on unrelenting pursuit with strong reserves,
in order finally to destroy the repeatedly defeated army
with an abundant harvest of victories.   Therefore, he tried
to storm with the *small* forces that brought him victory at
Chancellorsville the similar position at Gettysburg, in order
to have *all of the remainder* of his army rested and available
for reckless pursuit.

The assault failed! It would probably have been possible
to win a victory after heavy sacrifices with a strong concentration of all corps, but the main purpose, the conquest
of the North, and thereby the forcing of peace, would have
been unrealized. "I can not sacrifice one more man without
decisive results," he said. "My soldiers are too valuable
for that. It is *peace* for which we are fighting!"

In my opinion it would not have been difficult at Gettysburg to maneuver General Meade out of his formidable
position either by marching vigorously to the north or east,
whereby the seaports would have been threatened, or, if this
seemed too risky with possible danger to the alternative of
retreat, by advancing upon Frederickstown and threatening
Washington. But excessive disdain for the enemy, who
fought better, however, in his own country than anywhere
else, caused the simplest plan of a direct attack upon the
position at Gettysburg to prevail and deprived the army of
victory.

In view of these circumstances, nobody can blame General
Meade for not being convinced of victory until the Southerners had withdrawn, and even then for following the
intact army cautiously in order not to lose the fruits of

victory by a mistake, for which his opponent was constantly watching.

It was decided to retreat at noon, July 4. The wagon trains started moving early, the army not until toward evening, and the march continued through the night. Since my horse was weak, I attached myself to the infantry, and after it had rained and stormed constantly on roads most impassable, I arrived with the infantry, drenched and frozen, at Fairfield, where I lay down in the grass and let my exhausted horse graze. General Lee likewise soon arrived, burdened with anxiety over munitions, prisoners, the wounded, and the wagon trains, since the rain would not stop. Also, we promptly received the report that the ford was no longer passable because of the rising of the Potomac, and that our pontoon bridges at Falling Water had been partly destroyed by a raiding party. We had no pontoons with the army. Likewise, our long train, which was accompanied by only a few squadrons, was attacked by a large detachment of cavalry. Infantry was able to save everything here, and thus the enterprising quartermaster (the officer who commanded the train) rallied about 250 teamsters, mostly semi-invalid soldiers, who took their guns out of the wagons and not only successfully beat off the attack, but also took several prisoners.

On the same day, July 5, the main body of troops started out and went as far as the mountains, whereby only very few exhausted soldiers were to be seen, although many of the men were barefooted, and the spirit was so extraordinary that the weary troops received the old general with enthusiastic cheers, despite the retreat and deluded hopes. Sincere calls, such as "Old Lee is still alive! Now all is well!" etc., expressed the true sentiments of the men. I can truly say that nothing in the South touched and moved me more than the faithfulness of these thoroughly drenched, muddy, and ragged warriors to their noble leader in the disappointment of defeat. We moved into a wet camp at night, in the open as always at this time.

We arrived at Hagerstown on the morning of the 6th,

where we remained until July 10, camping in a beautiful little forest. From here I rode at the General's request to the Potomac, where the engineers, with the sappers who had just been mustered, were to rebuild the parts of the bridge destroyed by the Northerners and to construct the urgently needed bridge. Reconnaissance soon showed that the trees standing by the river were mostly oaks, which are not suitable for floats and are too hard to work for the quick completion of other structures. On the other hand, several sawmills were discovered, which provided a sufficient supply of boards and crossbeams. A section of bridge about 300 feet in length was entirely gone. Thus the decision was made to build new pontoons with slanting front and rear, 30 feet long on top and 18 feet on the bottom, 7 feet wide on top and 6 feet on the bottom. Altogether, 15 new pontoons were built, 7 old ones were repaired, the bridge floor for the 300 feet was built, the pontoons were caulked with oakum picked from old rope and were tarred at the seams, and stone anchors and wooden crossbeams were made. All of the material for the bridge about 800 feet long was floated downstream five and three-fourths miles ["5/4 deutsche Meilen"] and assembled as a bridge in 68 hours, counted from the beginning of the work, whereby it is to be noted that the men and the officers were not acquainted with one another, rain poured down all the time, and there was such a shortage of tools that a squad had to be content with an ax, a saw, and chisel.[19]

General Lee stopped at Hagerstown and waited to see what Meade would do. Meade did nothing.

The General once said to me at the close of a conversation: "Captain, we do our duty in good conscience according to our best judgement and to the best of our ability. Providence alone grants the victory. In its hands I calmly place our fate on the day of battle!"[20]

[19] See Freeman, III, 137, for the story of Scheibert's bridge-building experience.

[20] Compare Scheibert's "As soon as I order the troops forward into battle, I lay the fate of my army in the hands of God" (*Der Bürgerkrieg* . . . , p. 39). See Freeman, II, 347, n. 146; III, 140; and Fremantle, p. 80.

In these days I drew a map for General Stuart and again lived happily with his pleasant staff. The genial Colonel Fremantle, who was respected by all, left us to ride through the outposts to the North and was kind enough to carry news from me to my parents and my fiancée in Europe, to whom I had been unable to send a letter in four months.[21]

Since the enemy was gradually coming nearer, from six to eight miles of trenches were thrown up around our camp on the 11th, which seemed to me to be too extensive for 70,000 men, since there were about four men to a pace. But Colonel [A. L.] Long of the staff said with a laugh: "Any breastwork within itself amounts to a defense of ten men to a pace, for since Fredericksburg the Yankees have tremendous respect for these trenches." A battle was expected on this day and on the 12th, since the Northerners were feeling us out.

These were unhappy days for our General. First came the very depressing news of the fall of Vicksburg; then the Potomac rose so much that all contact with the base came to an end; and finally came the news that the General's brave son, General W. H. Lee, had been taken from the arms of his wife, despite his severe wounds, and had been carried to Washington as a prisoner, and that the Northern government threatened to hang him at the slightest dissatisfaction with the behavior of the South.[22]

A character like that of General Lee would not bow before such misfortune. Indeed, he was lively on the morning of the 13th, even cheerful in the thought that Meade would attack him, which he seemed most ardently to desire. "Captain, for once we can receive him here behind defensive works," he said cheerfully. "Then our poor boys will not need to attack unprotected through the hottest fire, as they have always done!" The fact that this hope also came to naught was quite disconcerting to him, although he had not been perturbed by all of the misfortune. For on the same

---

[21] *Ibid.*, pp. 146-150. Fremantle left July 9 and arrived in New York City July 12.
[22] See Freeman, III, 139, 210-211, 216-217; Chesney, II, 119.

afternoon came reports that the enemy had likewise dug in opposite us on the other bank of the Antietam. "That is too long for me; I can not wait for that," he said, and turning to me, he added, "What do you think about that, Captain? They have but little courage!"

Thus the retreat was ordered on the 14th, and it began suddenly, since the Potomac had subsided for the moment and could now be forded. Men rode along all of the lines now as if to reconnoiter, so that neither the troops nor the enemy would be made aware of anything, and then the move was begun quickly and secretly, but the outposts were not withdrawn until night.

It rained constantly during the crossing, and the weather was bitter cold and unpleasant. In view of this, the infantry and the artillery went across the bridge, the wagon trains and the cavalry went through the ford, and the ambulances, the staffs, etc., were brought across on two old ferries. But the worst was the fact that the roads south of the river were so miserable that the wheels sank down to the axles, and they were so congested that no one could walk along beside the vehicles. The night was pitch-black. One could not see his hand before his face. Men would fall. They would get between the wagons, and the horses would get in the ditch or would come to a stop at some places. Here a person was shoved, and there he shoved someone else, so that everything collided in the ice-cold rain, which might have confused and disturbed things, but all proceeded in order and with only slight delays, although horses and men suffered alike in the process. The military machine generated little friction and was maneuverable and running well as a result of constant operation in war.[23]

A fire was built for light at a crossroad, where especially great confusion might arise, and the General stood here with us throughout the night to regulate and enliven the march, to keep all in high spirits and on the track.

---

[23] Freeman, III, 140ff. "Lee's prayers seemed answered on the 13th" because "a good bridge" had at last been laid across the Potomac at Williamsport by "resourceful Major J. A. Harman."

Since the army was safely across the river on the next morning, and thus the campaign was probably ended for a long time, I carried out my long nurtured decision to go by way of Richmond to Charleston, for the siege of which, according to all newspapers, the Northerners were making most extensive preparations, and thus to *say farewell to the respected Army of Northern Virginia.*[24]

Therefore, I took leave of the gentlemen of the staff, unfortunately without being able to see the General himself, and leaving my pack behind, which I gave to the Negroes, I set out on the way to Richmond with my lame horse, which had one shoe missing. On the same day I rode to Winchester, arriving in the rain at night with a young courier. We found all of the houses closed and no inhabitant ready to admit us. Since I was overtaken by weariness, and while the young man was looking for the house of an acquaintance, I decided to hitch my horse to a broken gas lamp post, and then I lay down on the sidewalk and let the rain water flow past me, ready to fall asleep at any moment. The courier also came back without having achieved his purpose, and he was on the point of sharing my soaked bed with me when the door of a house near us opened and a lady appeared with a light in her hand. My bedfellow ran over and asked for a small space in the hall, but the lady was kind enough to give us rooms with beds. I owe the food for my very hungry horse and my friendly reception on the following day, in spite of the bad odor given off by my dirty clothes, to my bungling facility in playing the piano, which was gazed upon with astonishment in the quite unmusical South.

I left toward noon and went to a blacksmith shop, but only by pulling the bellows for hours in the absence of a helper was I able toward evening to induce the deluged smith to shoe my horse. I had to pay the smith two paper dollars for nailing the shoe to the hoof after I had by chance found one that would fit.

---

[24] Ross left for Richmond on July 24 (*op. cit.*, p. 103); it may be supposed that Scheibert left shortly afterwards, for the two met again within a few days.

I rode alone into the lovely Valley of Virginia, happy as usual and at peace with God. The country is called Virginia because nature there is of such virginal purity, and because the young women are nowhere more beautiful, more modest, or more natural than in this paradiasical valley.

The Shenandoah, which is about 200 paces wide, runs along the valley, murmuring over the rocks, bordered by magnolias, oaks, beeches, walnut trees, and the splendid "willows," which are unknown in our country, and which we know only as maimed dwarves.

These beautiful, large trees incline their heads so that they meet and thus form a high, beautiful, majestic hall over the murmuring, resonant stream. Here one rides along the wonderful edge of the woods and along cliffs, and there a farm home that has been burned indicates its former splendor. Curious people or beautiful women look out of the verandas of farm homes that are still standing, and children whom Rubens would have taken as models play by the road. The various chains of the Allegheny Mountains in the distance form the blue, misty background.

On the first day I rode as far as Middletown, where I met a Rev. Dr. Deems from Wilson, North Carolina, a good, religious gentleman and an equally talented speaker. We joined each other after our first conversation, since destiny led us along the same road. He had been with the army to investigate the fate of his mortally wounded and captured son. A saddle bag on the minister's horse, with a ham in one half and in the other our bread, a fresh supply of which we obtained at the various farms, was the repository of our provisions, for this saddle bag contained all of the meals of the two of us, which we ate at beautiful springs in the shade while our horses were grazing, and we would light a fire in the flowering meadow to warm our limbs and to rejoice our hearts.

Here I must remark that the Southern cavalry (also the artillery and the staffs) would immediately unsaddle their horses as soon as they came to a camping place and would either send them out to graze on fenced pasture or would order a few Negroes to take care of them. The officers' servants and some teamsters and convoy soldiers were Negroes, to be sure, but *not a single Negro* bore arms at that time. (One must judge accordingly all of the beautiful "lying true stories" in feuilletons, etc., where female spies, etc., hold forth in long observations about the mistreatment of Negro soldiers in the South.) These blacks were treated very well. When I once spoke of "Niggers," I was even admonished that it was preferable not to use this derogatory word for these people, who were of low intelligence, to be sure, but who were very useful, and I was told that it was a Yankee word.

Thus we rode by way of Strasburg, Woodstock, Mount Jackson, New Market, Harrisonburg, and Mt. Crawford to Staunton, where my companion introduced me to the very modest family of the attorney Kayser in his home and aroused a sensation by preaching a fine sermon for which he had been given the text only an hour before beginning.

This ride was so instructive and pleasant for me that I still have a feeling of sincere gratitude toward the Valley and the doctor. We finally went to Richmond, where general dejection prevailed, and therefore, after the retreat was over, the President proclaimed a day of general prayer and penitence, which General Lee announced to the army. . . .[25]

. . . .

In Richmond I parted with the amiable clergyman, my companion, took a bath, and put on clean clothes, a business, the full comfort of which one learns to appreciate only after months of dirtiness. To my great joy, my friend, Captain Ross, who likewise intended to leave the army, happened to come out of an opposite room a few days later when I was working with my door open. Von Borcke, who was still suffering very much with his wound, since his breathing was especially difficult, was the third member of the group each day until Mr. Lawley, who was diligently collecting

[25] This proclamation of July 25, 1863 may be seen in James D. Richardson (ed.), *Compilation of the Messages and Papers of the Confederacy* . . . (Nashville, 1906), I, 328.

materials for the *Times,* also became associated with us. A young French consul likewise joined us, and thus five great powers, jovially called the "Congress," dined at Madame Zitelli's, where England's, France's, Prussia's, Austria's, and America's interests found their cheerful representatives.[26] I visited the previously mentioned ministers again and studied in the Office of Engineers the siege of Vicksburg, without obtaining thereby any especially note-worthy information.[27]

Most interesting to me was a visit at the home of President Jefferson Davis. I had already called upon him once, but this important gentleman then expressed his sincere regrets about his inability to receive me, since he was ill, and he invited me to repeat the visit, which I did one evening. The servant, a Negro of refined manners, in frock coat and white tie, received me with great propriety and was about to announce me to the President.

Since I heard voices in the room, I asked him to tell the President to be kind enough to receive me in private audience, since I only wished to get acquainted with him and did not wish to leave without having seen him. Moreover, I was constrained to make this request because of my dress, which, far from being a black frock coat, was more appropriate for travel than for the drawing room.

But hardly had I entered the elegant door when the head of the Confederacy stood before me, extended both hands, and greeted me warmly and cordially as a friend of General Lee. He escorted me thereby into the adjoining room, where a large group was assembled, to whom I was immediately introduced. The President, a gentleman in whose company one feels at ease after the first moments, and whose conversation was that of an important man, told me that General Lee had been kind enough to mention me in a

[26] *Ibid.,* p. 104. Ross spent ten or twelve days in Richmond at the Ballard House, where he, Scheibert, Lawley, Borcke, and the "young French consul"—representing "five great powers"— shared their "jovial 'Congress'."
[27] In Chapter I, pp. 31-32, Scheibert mentions having met Secretary Seddon, Colonel Jeremy F. Gilmer and other officers in the Confederate Engineer Bureau.

respectful manner, and he soon turned the conversation to the most recent events.[28] He questioned me in detail about my opinion of the expedition, as well as about the troops, and he expressed himself in quite measured terms concerning the course of the campaign and the fall of Vicksburg. He listened with interest to my opinion about the army, and he showed himself in society, as well as in private conversation, to be an energetic man, full of humanitarianism, and a true Christian. The conversation became more general, and, among other things, it turned to the destruction of the President's estates on the Mississippi, whereby a lady lamented the forceful removal and destruction of the President's famous library. He said that he demanded a sacrifice of property and blood of every Confederate, even of the lowliest, and for this reason he had not a word to waste about such trifles, but if he pitied anything, it was his poor Negroes, who had been living at his home for generations and had now been driven off to the North and abandoned to misery and ruin. He said that he had a personal interest in every one of them.

The discussion also turned to two captured Federal captains who had also been selected to die by the noose as revenge for two Confederate officers of like rank who had been unjustly hanged. When the time for the execution would come, the President had always postponed it from month to month, in spite of the pressure of public opinion.

He said on this occasion, when the exchange of prisoners was also being discussed, that it was his endeavor so far as possible to keep this war within the limits of humanity, since war is by nature barbaric. He told me that he likewise assumed a position of states' rights in politics, and he also discussed the conflict in a manner just as calm and unimpassioned as statesmanlike.

His religious sentiment, his irreproachable conduct, his unselfishness and firmness, as well as his great talent and

[28] In *Mit Schwert und Feder*, p. 154, written many years later, Scheibert stated that Davis asked him in this interview to enlist help for the Confederacy from Emperor Napoleon. See Introduction, pp. 12-13.

culture, were expressed on all occasions in his deeds and in his proclamations.

The fact that an uncritical, partisan madness now besmirches his character, that the rabble scorns him, can not rob him of the place in history which will be given him when calm reason stands in judgment over blind confusion. To praise him now with prospect of success is just as hopeless as it was to make anything intelligible to the populace with cold concepts and calm logic during the French Revolution.

The President looked sickly, and his hair had grayed to some extent within the previous year. Let his photograph be compared with that of the murdered President Lincoln, and one will see from the features of the two that the former was a more important man and thinker, which a careful consideration of their deeds will also confirm.

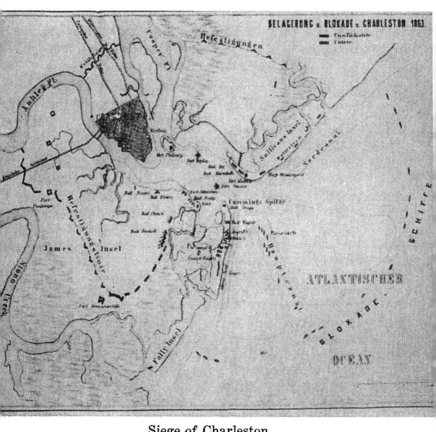

Siege of Charleston

CHAPTER VI

Siege of Charleston

A PAUSE OF EXHAUSTION had come over the extreme efforts in the theater of war in Virginia during my stay in Richmond.

Only in Carolina were the Northerners stirring, now seriously to begin the siege of Charleston that had already been projected once.

Earlier attempts had failed. Even the ironclads had not proved their reputation of invincibility, as we shall later see, and all of the intelligence and industrial activity of resourceful New England were now to be called upon to conquer the point of origin of the rebellion. Therefore, public and private factories vied with one another in the manufacture of siege guns, and ironclad vessels were constructed according to the newest models. New, rifled cannon of formidable make were to be tried, lighting machines were to be tested, and armored vessels were to be matched against torpedoes. Little wonder that America and Europe looked forward with excitement to the struggle, and that I also approached the siege with almost feverish expectation. But back to the subject. After the difficult trip by railroad from Richmond to Charleston, on which Captain Ross most cordially accompanied me before he left for the Army of Tennessee, we arrived in Charleston, which I found to be considerably more desolate than upon my first arrival there, and we were all the more surprised, therefore, to find Mill's House, the first hotel of the Confederacy, in full flourish. Naturally, we took lodging in it. I want to remark immediately that this hotel had the best service of any tavern with which I became acquainted in the South, even during the later bombardment of Charleston, when the last inhabitants disconcertedly left the city.[1]

Immediately after my arrival I reported to General Beauregard and to Colonel [David B.] Harris, Chief of Engineers, who granted me access to the offices and maps, which I was naturally not permitted to copy.

My principal place of residence was Fort Johnson, where my friend lived, Captain [John] Howard of the Engineers, who always received me as hospitably as possible in his frame houses, which were riddled with shell, and who facilitated considerably my inspection of the defense with his ready and obliging help.

Fort Johnson was the most interesting point of the forward terrain, since it was possible here to survey Fort Sumter and Fort Wagner (the two main objectives of the attack), the steamers of the fleet, and the monitors, and, from an observation post nearby, to get a bird's-eye view of the entire field of attack.

Fort Sumter was so near that the effect of every shot that hit it could be observed accurately, since we were almost beneath the trajectory of the shells. From this observation point we also had an opportunity to ride over all of James Island, for Captain Howard not only directed the mounting of all of the batteries on this place, but he was also sufficiently provided with horses, mules, etc., to give a friend a mount.

From this point I shall give a picture of the execution of the attack and of the defense as it appeared to me, to the extent that I was able to observe it with the means at my disposal.

The first ride convinced me that the defense had not been idle since my presence in March, and that it had set up a number of batteries.

---

[1] Ross, pp. 104-106, describes their trip from Richmond to Charleston on August 6 as "very disagreeable." According ·to him the Mill's House was "very hot and dusty and rather knocked up."

But before we enter upon the events, the reader must take a look at the map of Charleston [p. 129] and must learn that James Island, so far as it is firm, as well as the entire East Coast here, is covered with leafy and flowering vegetation so luxuriant and magnificent that the like of it is not to be seen again anywhere in these regions. On this terrain, which extends about five miles in width along the sea, mostly in the form of low islands, grows the famous sea-island cotton, which knows no equal.

These islands are separated from the sea by impenetrable swamps, by lagoons, and by a strip of quite narrow island dunes bordering directly on the sea, on which only sand vegetation grows. Examples are Folly Island, Morris Island, Sullivan's Island, etc. The real defense included the fortification of the firm sea islands, so that the swamps and lagoons served as frontal obstacles. Advanced batteries and forts on the dune islands held the blockading fleet at a respectable distance. Most important of these strongholds were Fort Wagner, built in 1862-1863 of dune sand and provided with bombproof rooms, and Fort Moultrie, with its circular wall of masonry.

In addition to the batteries, the inner defense of the harbor was served by Fort Sumter (a pentagonal fort of three levels, constructed of brick), Fort Johnson, which was an earthwork that was easily thrown up, the palm wood structure of Fort Ripley, and Fort Pinckney, with its circular wall of masonry.

The fortified lines consisted of open flèches, and of closed redoubts in the second line, between which there were extensive abatis. The forts located on the sea islands, between the batteries, such as Fort Pemberton and Fort Secessionville, suffered because they were too small and because the lines were too short.

So far as the attack itself is concerned, the Federals had already decided to take James Island by a quick surprise attack in July, 1862, and they had also tried this in vain with a few ships and monitors, as I shall call the armored gunboats with one cannon for the sake of brevity.

After this event, the press, and thereby public opinion of the North America, had talked itself into the prejudiced opinion that the ironclads, which had indeed already shown their efficiency, especially against wooden men-of-war, could accomplish all possible things in the world and could especially *"conquer Charleston independently."* Therefore, an attack with ironclads alone was attempted in April of this year.

The somewhat obscure intention was to raze Fort Sumter with gunfire in a few hours and then, unconcerned with the fire of the other batteries, which were indeed stronger than Sumter, to steam to the city in order to fire it with shells, and then to take it.

For this purpose seven monitors deployed before Fort Sumter, outside the harbor, and began a bombardment of the fort that continued for several hours, whereby the 7-pounder, rifled Parrotts and the 15-pounder columbiads knocked large holes through the masonry, which was five feet thick. Then the *Weehawken* was sent forward to sound and to reconnoiter the entrance to the harbor. It steamed to within 800 feet of Fort Sumter and brought the report that the blades of the propeller had become entangled in cables, etc., a false report, since neither cables nor anything else then lay at the place where the *Weehawken* had ended its reconnaissance. Moreover, another monitor, the *Keokuk*, was sunk by the 10-pounder columbiads and the 7-pounder, rifled cannon of the fort, so that the fleet of ironclads withdrew after a battle lasting about six hours and abandoned the idea of taking up the fight alone with a marine fortification.

Now General [Q. A.] Gilmore, who had already conquered Fort Pulaski at Savannah with quick energy in 1861, was sent against Charleston, and he combined a land and sea attack against Fort Wagner and Fort Sumter, still placing too much confidence in the armored fleet against land batteries. The advantage of armored ships, which is by no means to be underestimated, lies in their superiority over wooden

ships and in their characteristic of being able to pass close
to the most formidable batteries almost with impunity.

In August, 1863, General Gilmore suddenly attacked
weakly defended Folly Island, which he seized with the first
onslaught, and soon thereafter he effected a lodgment on
Morris Island, which he used as the base for his regular
attack on For Wagner. For support, in a sense as flanking,
enfilading, and mobile batteries, he had six monitors of best
construction, each with one 15-pounder, smoothbore columbiad, and the armored frigate *Ironsides*, which carried eight
rifled, 9-pounder Parrotts. Moreover, the blockade fleet
was at his disposal for bombardments, etc.[2]

The first offensive action on Morris Island had just begun
when I arrived in Charleston, and batteries had immediately
been constructed which fired upon Fort Sumter at a distance
of 7,000 paces, and which scored hits against the rear of
the fort with about sixty percent of the shots, inasmuch as
an average of two out of three shells struck the masonry.
This bombardment was also continued at night while a
calcium light set up on a ship from 2,000 to 3,000 feet away
lighted Fort Sumter so well that every stone could be seen
from Fort Johnson. In Fort Sumter, where the forepart
had been sandbagged after the attack in April, and where
guns had been moved from casements into batteries, they
began to secure the rear casements, intended for officers
quarters and guard rooms, against the murderous fire of
the attacking 200-300-pounder rifles as soon as it became
obvious that Morris Island was the field of operations.
Therefore, they first attempted to cover the entire rear side
with sandbags containing about one and a half bushels of
sand. The existing masonry wharves afforded a good
foundation for this work, but since it was necessary to
transport the sand from Sullivan's Island to the fort at
night on steamships under the fire of the batteries, after
the courtyard had already been emptied to water level, this

[2] For a detailed account of the attacks on Charleston see Alfred
Roman, *Military Operations of General Beauregard* (New York, 1884),
II, 66ff., and John Johnson, *Defense of Charleston Harbor* . . . 1863-
1865 (Charleston, 1890).

plan was given up, and only the casemated rooms were lined as much as possible with sand and rubbish.

The powder magazines were in the two rear corners, which were for this reason constructed of walls eight feet thick. Nevertheless, they were strengthened with walls ten to twelve feet thick, since it was not possible to get wrought iron in time. Thus the corners were surrounded by about twenty feet of masonry. Still, it was later necessary to get the powder out at night, for the enemy shells threatened to penetrate the interior and to blow up the entire fort.

The shots, first at a distance of 7,000 feet, and later coming nearer and nearer with the batteries, were 200- to 300-pound balls, percussion shells, and also antipersonnel shrapnel. The balls shook the entire wall, while the percussion shells blasted holes from which the sand trickled. Nevertheless, the brave garrison held out behind the heaps of rubbish, despite daily wounds and deaths. Although the shells had great and astonishing results against the masonry of Fort Sumter, they had little effect on Wagner Battery, which was constructed with an expenditure of much money and effort.

The Federals had observed, to be sure, that the individual batteries, and even the ironclads, could accomplish nothing against Wagner Battery, which was actually constructed of sand. It was decided, therefore, to sweep the battery from the face of the earth in a combined artillery attack by sea and land. Again I had the good fortune on the morning of August 17 to be in Fort Johnson, where I could observe the battle.

Six monitors, each with one 15-pounder columbiad, an armored frigate with eight 10-pounder columbiads, six steam-powered men-of-war, each with twelve to twenty and more guns, which stayed beyond the range of the fire of the fort, and all batteries of the land attack with about thirty-six cannon opened a bombardment at six o'clock in the morning, in which, therefore, about a hundred and eighty guns of monstrous caliber participated. The sight was really tremendous. The fifteen-pound, hollow shells, which penetrated deeply into the breastworks, threw the soil up like mines in columns thirty to fifty feet high. The projectiles that were flying past sent up sprays of water in cascades which were high at first, and which then gradually diminished. Everything was enveloped in foam and dust. It seemed as if the entire fort were disintegrating and disappearing completely from the earth to fly away into dusty chaos. The hissing of the shells, the sharp cracking of the exploding bombs and shrapnel, the whirring of the fragments, and the dull roar and rumble of the cannon all did their part in making the picture lively and interesting. We were all in worried suspense over the gallant garrison of the battery, which had already heroically repelled two strong attacks, and we believed, to judge by visible effects, that they were facing destruction. The cannonading lasted five hours, in the course of which Wagner, Gregg, and Sumter replied weakly, while our battery on James Island attempted to disturb the attacking batteries on Morris Island as much as possible. But how astounded we were when six of the seven cannons opened fire again as soon as the armored vessels withdrew from the front. The damages to the battery had been repaired in one night, and thus nothing had been accomplished by the bombardment, although the bombproof room had been shaken repeatedly.

Fort Wagner and Gregg Battery were voluntarily evacuated at night on September 5, when the zigzag offensive operations had progressed approximately to the escarpment.

An assault which the Federals undertook against Fort Sumter in boats on September 9 was thrown back by the garrison of the fort, which was defending itself only in rubble. The defenders did not put up a heavy fire, but they used rocks at night, which they rained on the heads of the landing troops, and not only did they victoriously repel the attack, but they also captured 107 men and nine boats, as well as the Union flag which had floated over Fort Sumter before the war, and which was to wave there again in the future.

Thus ended the battle on Morris Island, which showed

that sand batteries are to be preferred above all others, so far as *resistance to shells* is concerned, although their *invulnerability* can be effected only by ingenious means and audacious defense, unless moats hinder the attack. The battle also showed that bold courage is the best defensive weapon.

One more fact should be mentioned. When the attack on Morris Island had progressed to within 600 feet of Fort Wagner, the Federals attempted to establish themselves permanently in the swamps that lie between Morris and James Islands. Therefore, the grievous work of mounting a battery here was undertaken and carried out. This was accomplished by making a road with brush, etc., through the swamp to the emplacement at night. Sandbags, which formed the breastworks, were brought to the emplacement during the night, while a cannon (a 200-pounder) was dragged over on boards. Although this cannon was about four and a half miles from Charleston, it was still able to bombard the city, so that the shells reached the center of the city. The barrel was intrenched at an angle of from four to five degrees for this purpose, as we heard, since no gun carriage could withstand the recoil. The shells were filled with Greek fire.[3]

This notorious "Greek" fire consisted at that time of turpentine with incendiary material, and it did no damage, since very few of the shells exploded, but it did make a very loud noise, which sounded even less pleasant in view of the fact that the bombardment began suddenly and unexpectedly at one o'clock in the night and aroused the inhabitants of the city, including many women and children, from a safe sleep. The result of the bombardment was that the few remaining families left the city in fear, that a house had a hole torn in it, and that a small boy broke his leg. Moreover, the first cannon burst after some twenty shots, the second one likewise during the following night, and the swamp battery

[3] This was the "Swamp Angel," the "most famous gun in the Civil War" (see Miller, ed., V, 110).

did not go into action again in my time, that is, up to September 22.

If we now consider more closely all of the results prior to this date, the Federals had only captured Morris Island, had constructed a small battery in the swamp, and had destroyed Fort Sumter's capacity for active resistance. In general, therefore, they were still three and a half to four and a half miles from the stronghold, and if they were to continue the attack that had been launched, they still had to work their way through the swamp to James Island in order to be nearer to the city. To be sure, the city had ceased to be a commercial town, since the running of the blockade was made much more difficult even by the seizing of Morris Island, and since all tradesmen had also left the city.

This made it possible at the same time to withdraw a part of the blockading fleet. The use of torpedoes led to no results in Charleston, while an experiment succeeded in seriously damaging the frigate *Ironsides* with an exceedingly simply constructed submarine boat.[4] I shall give a brief critique to explain again the nature of the siege and to clarify the general results.

The general plan of *attack* was a bungled one, because it was based on hypotheses that could haunt the minds only of military amateurs. Too much confidence had been placed in the ironclads, and their main attack was to be supported only by a secondary attack on Fort Sumter. It soon developed, however, that the attack on Morris Island was becoming the cardinal point, while the armored fleet fell to secondary rank and assumed in the attack the role that our lighter, mobile batteries will play in future sieges. Therefore, Fort Wagner was not taken until the *land attack* reached the battery, and Fort Sumter had *by no means* fallen at that time.

If the armored fleet were really to attain great results, it would have to act with absolute audacity, as we have

---

[4] See Albert Kelln, "Confederate Submarines," *Virginia Magazine of History and Biography*, LXI, 293-303 (July, 1953), and Wm. Stanley Hoole, "Alabama-Built Submarine Was First to Sink a Battleship," *Birmingham News Monthly Mazagine*, Dec. 13, 1953, pp. 12-13.

remarked above, as Admiral Farragut acted when he went up the Mississippi between the forts and took New Orleans.

If a land attack was really necessary, it would have been wiser if Charleston had been blockaded and besieged with somewhat more troops from the land side, whereby there would have been realized at the same time the great advantage of cutting it off from land sources of personnel and material aid, while, as things were, it was completely open to the rear and, like Titan, was able to draw new strength from its mother, the country.

Therefore, the great expectations that had been called forth were illusory.

Only the following things were noteworthy: 1. Masonry is a poor defensive material. 2. Earth is still the best material for breastworks. 3. Even ironclad vessels play only a secondary role against land fortifications. 4. Torpedoes are mainly a *psychological* weapon, since no enemy vessel dared enter the harbor, although the few torpedoes that were laid there had in many cases become useless and were declared by the defenders themselves to be "humbugs." They were important in *rivers*.

Furthermore, the first use of large, rifled calibers at long ranges, the illumination of targets at night, and the practical construction of the Confederate earthworks were interesting.

The greater part of Charleston was deserted during the siege. Only in the northern part, where many Germans and Irishmen also reside, were a few people still at home.

Everything was frightfully expensive except board at the hotel. A bottle of wine cost up to 24 paper dollars (graybacks), a pair of boots 60 dollars, a suit, coat, trousers, and vest, 220 dollars. A dinner for seven people, with red wine and a few courses, coffee, etc., cost 770 paper dollars.

Fortunately, one gold dollar was worth two and a half paper dollars at first and ten paper dollars in the last part of the time.

I lived in Mill's House with Captain Ross, whose calm judgment made him an estimable and amiable travel companion. He observed the siege with interest and was later with General Longstreet in the campaign in Tennessee (Battle of Chattanooga) after I had left. I also became acquainted with Frank Vizetelly ["Visitelli"], the sketchman for the *Illustrated London News,* who is well-known in England, who had been before Sebastopol and in China, and who was present in the campaign in Italy in 1859 and landed in 1860 with Garibaldi, from whom he had received and was holding several letters.[5]

One night Ross came into my room and said, "The city is being bombarded. A bomb-shell must have just fallen in our section!" I laughed skeptically, and we both looked out of the window. Vizetelly appeared a few minutes later, out of breath, and said that a bomb had just struck his hotel and had gone into the opposite corner of the house. We dressed and went with curiousity to the shore. And indeed, we saw a flicker of light from time to time on the horizon and could then count to "16" without hearing anything, when a buzzing would begin, becoming stronger and stronger, and finally becoming so intense, especially at night, that we believed we were at "32," that the shot was coming straight toward us, while it was really roaring far away and would fall somewhere in a garden or in some street. In such moments most of the occupants would creep foolishly into the houses, where the effect of the bombs is much more dangerous.

We noticed that each successive shot fell shorter, landing in another section of the city, with the last ones all falling too short and hitting, therefore, harmlessly in the harbor. We did not even get out of bed on the following nights. Since the fuse was at the leading end of the shells, their trajectory could be observed very well, and the graceful curve marked their track very beautifully in the dark sky.[6]

In addition to the officers, we had become acquainted with

---

[5] Ross and Vizetelly also describe the bombardment of Charleston. The two men left together for Chattanooga on September 14 (Ross, pp. 108-117; Hoole, pp. 86-99).
[6] Scheibert omits the amusing story of the Vizetelly-Ross betting during the bombardment (see Ross, pp. 118-120; Hoole, pp. 94-98).

the French, Spanish, and English consuls, with whom our dealings were very pleasant. The proprietors who had remained in the city also tried to make our stay as pleasant as possible, despite their limited economy, and they did their utmost to show us how pleased they were with our presence and with our interest in their struggle and in their cause.

Since I am now almost at the end of my life in the war, and since many of my readers are doubtless curious to look into a plantation, I interrupt the fire of the siege for a short time and invite them to accompany me on this peaceful expedition.

On September 1, Ross and I accepted the friendly invitation of Colonel Bull to accompany him to his plantation at Ashley Hall, which was managed entirely by his Negroes in his absence. Since we would not miss anything in Charleston, we drove upstream along the right bank of the Ashley River in a buggy, through a luxuriant forest, where thick underbrush with wet ditches and the vegetation, now more luxuriant than ever, offered us a continual change.

All sorts of flowers, among them a strikingly purple one, the blossoms of which were set cylindrically on a stem like fuchsia, mingled with the magnificent green, from which the tall bamboo cane stretched forth its neck from time to time, and over which towered the huge live oaks, a hardwood, from the limbs of which hung dainty Spanish moss like graceful fringes. Fields of rice and cotton attracted our attention. We saw the famous sea-island cotton, which is worth almost twice as much as the short-staple cotton that is grown in the country. The former is considerably more sensitive to weather than the latter. It must be more carefully cultivated, and it grows only along the unhealthy, swampy seacoast.

The blooming cypresses looked very beautiful. Little white flowers without stamen were fixed in the green like small myrtle flowers in a bouquet. Pretty rose-red, beautifully shaped mushrooms and strange, lilac-colored, yellow, and blue flowers blocked our way at the side paths and caused us to walk slowly. We returned loaded with flowers to our coach.

We finally arrived at the plantation home, which was built in simple Old English style in the middle of a meadow by the river. The largest live oaks that I have ever seen, with shades measuring 280 feet, stood on the short, fresh, and succulently lustrous grass.

The house did not look as elegant from the outside as most of the larger plantation homes, but it looked very simple, since it is one of the oldest in Carolina. On the other hand, everything was very comfortably arranged on the inside.

The Negroes lived entirely to themselves in small, white houses, as was generally the case thereabout, and as is customary, they kept chickens and swine, and they led a merry life, since the Colonel lived in the city most of the time. There was naturally much cause for reproof.

A stroll in the flower-garden was immediately rewarded with unusually sweet, though hard-skinned, reddish grapes, while the white ones had softer skins and were so large that one grape made almost half a wineglassful of juice.

These are the domestic varieties which I found everywhere, and which have a future if they are cultivated, for even now the juice from the press tastes similar to a Madeira that is not very sweet. I brought along to Europe as curiosities small melons that are put in the linen, and gourds, from which drinking vessels can be carved. The paths in the garden that was located picturesquely along the Ashley River, at the corners of which were immense aloes in vases, were lined with magnolias, chestnut trees, peach trees, lilac flowered acacia, and trees that were strange to me. A monument of an English governor, 1776, located in the middle of the garden, bore witness to the age of the estate. Elegantly bent bamboo cane that was twenty feet high indicated the swampy places in the garden. The small ponds in the garden were garlanded with oaks and willows, which were coquettishly reflected on the water, and on which osiers and grape vines were climbing, while the small fan palm that was two feet high spread its leaves close to the shore. The willow twigs and the Spanish moss let their fringes hang down toward the water like green, trickling drops.

The palmetto, as well as date and sago palms, reminded the visitor of the fact that he was in a tropical region, in case he should have doubted it for a moment.

At the risk of taking a plunge, we rowed in a rocking canoe the twenty paces to the cotton mill, one of which is found on every plantation and which makes gin cotton by removing the seed and the burs from the fruit by the very simple method of combing it. The misshapen wheels and axles, which had evidently been fashioned only with the help of axe and saw, were rotting during the war.

The owner's twelve year old son naturally went on a little hunt with us, when we shot a snow-white heron, for at this age the young cosmopolitan must already be able to ride horseback, to drive, and to shoot accurately. The young people also learn at an early age to wield the helm and the sail, and they show a remarkable knowledge of steam engineering, even in the South, which is for the most part without factories.[7]

When I observed that the siege of Charleston had come to a standstill, I considered returning home, and I went to Wilmington to get space on a blockade runner. Therefore, I paid farewell visits to the generals, to the Spanish Consul, Sr. Moncado, the French Consul, M. Lannon, and the English Consul, Mr. Pinkney Walker, as well as my other acquaintances, and I parted with regret from Captain Ross and the fine and good Captain Howard, to whom I was so greatly obliged in Charleston, for he advised me of every incident, notified me every time the batteries opened up, and provided me with horses and night quarters.

In Wilmington, which had been in enemy hands for a

[7] Ross, p. 112. Vizetelly did not accompany Scheibert and Ross to Ashley Hall, probably because he had already been entertained there in March, 1863 (see Hoole, pp. 74-77).

time,[8] one could observe the general demoralization that had been brought about by the turbulent state of affairs. The hotel had neither real service nor furniture. Two agreeable artists, the sculptor, Volks, and the painter, Robertson, accepted me as a third man in their room, but they soon left, whereupon I provided lodging in my room for two California lawyers, with whom I later ran the blockade. The many nights through which we fought in common the struggle against all imaginable species of pests for lack of mosquito nets quickly brought about a transitory comradeship in arms.

[8] Scheibert left Charleston for Wilmington early in mid-September, 1863. Wilmington did not fall into enemy hands until January 15, 1865.

CHAPTER VII

Return Voyage

GENERAL [W. H. C.] WHITING, Military Governor of North Carolina, upon whom I called, invited me to inspect the batteries along the Cape Fear River and the fortifications around Wilmington, which I did with great interest. A colonel of engineers accompanied me,[1] and I enriched my technical information essentially on this trip, especially since I became acquainted with a fort (Caswell) that was completely covered with iron bands, and observed a form of coastal batteries as practical as any that can be imagined.

A conversation with the General himself concerning past events was very stimulating, and the manner by which Fort Caswell had been built was quite interesting. The iron fort was constructed in view of the hostile fleet, so that the cannon had to be on the platform while the armor was being added above them. When two stations were finished, and when my traveling companion, the colonel of engineers who was supervising the construction, came to doubt the strength of this, his first iron structure, he pulled out his cannon and tested the iron bars of the roof with several shots at close range, first with a covering of one and a half feet of earth, while five feet of earth later covered the structure. After some minor changes, he found that his structure could hold out. This method seems to me to be

---

[1] This was undoubtedly Colonel William Lamb. See Thomas E. Taylor, *Running the Blockade* . . . (New York, 1896), pp. 55-59.

fully worthy of imitation in war, in case there are similar doubts.

Duty had dispelled all thoughts of going home up until this time. Now I decided to return home, and my thoughts drew me toward Europe.

Before I could leave—for we had to wait for a new moon—General Whiting invited me through his adjutant, Lieutenant [John S.] Fairly, who had taken a look at my desolate hotel, to spend the rest of the time in his abandoned camp. We rode into the charmingly located tent quarters, which were unoccupied at the moment, and which were shaded by old oak trees. From here we could see far across the islands and the sound and out onto the ocean.

There we two, with a few couriers and Negroes, lived the complete existence of a Robinson Crusoe, for only what was caught in the morning or evening appeared on the table, so that the meals always consisted of oysters, crabs, and fish, which our black servants were able to make into the most delicious soups, salads, and ragouts, boiled, baked, and broiled. Two beautiful Carolina women, who came flying along high and stately on horseback, interrupted the lonely, quiet life on the last day of my stay here. In the evening we cruised in the sound on sailboats with the ladies. While we were on the veranda in the beautiful moonlit night, under the Southern grape vines, and with the moon's disk reflecting in the sea and flooding the sound with peace, we chatted of house and home, of peace and war, and of the future. I rode to Wilmington on the next day.

When I was by chance walking along the shore there—I had already paid the owner of the ship a hundred and fifty dollars in gold for the three day voyage to Bermuda—I saw that my ship, the *A. D. Vance,* was just then weighing anchor and getting up steam to leave on that day, instead of the following day. I ran on board quickly, and the embarrassed captain confessed that he would have liked to leave without passengers, since they were an unpleasant, additional burden, and since the commander was determined to resist with force of arms any boarding of the vessel. He said that I might make the voyage with him, if I wanted to. I even received permission to fetch my baggage. When I hurried to the hotel, I happened to find my roommates in my room—two California lawyers, who had likewise booked passage. I told them the facts, and since the time was pressing, the three of us ran to the steamer, dragging our luggage or carrying it on our backs, and on the way we reported the departure to a few other fellow passengers, who also joined us. Hardly were we on board when the steamer got under way, and strange to say, with all of the twelve passengers that it had accepted. Even if our money had been refunded upon the departure of the steamer, we should still have been compelled to wait another month in the dull town of Wilmington, until the next new moon, and I should probably have arrived too late to take part in the campaign that followed in Schleswig.

The famous paddle wheeler *A. D. Vance*, the fastest steamer borne by the waves, carried us down the picturesque Cape Fear River. But at the mouth the pilot told us that the "bar" (reef at the pass) was too shallow, and that we would have to wait another week until high tide and the dark of the moon would come at the same time.

Thanks to the efforts of the Commander, Colonel [*sic*] Crossan,[2] the week spent in sight of the blockade fleet that was rocking on the horizon was most interesting. This ingenious gentleman, an officer of the former navy, and hence no blockade-running adventurer, but a man risking his life in the service of his native land, added life and cheer to the fine voyage. An enthusiastic admirer of Shakespeare, he stimulated discussions, gave lectures on him, and was able to keep a continual and lively conversation going about this author. There was music when the topic was concluded, or the well-known historiographer, Colonel [John H.] Wheeler of North Carolina, would read a treatise about the politics of this frequently controversial state. Often the

[2] A Captain Crossan, unidentified, is mentioned in *Official Records of the Union and Confederate Navies* . . . (Washington, 1903), 1 series, XVII, 872.

object of wit, this gentleman was capable of prompt re-
partee, and he finally became the subject of a humorous,
illustrated work by me, *Wheeleriana*, which was dedicated
to and later presented to the governor of his state. While
poetry, literature, music, and humor thus enlivened the ship
of evenings, morning brought with the help of the ship's
well-equipped boats an opportunity for sailing, angling,
fishing and strolling on the picturesque, virgin shores of
Cape Fear. Seventeen blockade-running steamers left and
eight entered while we were lying at the bar.

The pilot finally came! "It can be done today!" he said,
"To be sure, the water lacks a half foot of depth, but we
must risk it." When the moon was setting, we went as far
as the bar, beyond which we could see a boat with a light.
A buoy was dropped, the safety valve was weighted down,
and the fire was stoked so that the boiler was about to
burst. The wheels lashed the waves madly, and the steamer,
which was already flying as fast as an eagle, shot across
the water like an arrow. Then the bow rose high, the sides
of the ship bent, the ribs creaked and crackled, and the ship
was stuck in the sand as steady as a house. The two wheels
now alternately began their work of *back*-paddling, and
after an hour we floated back to the buoy. The dance began
anew. The hard thrust that took us straight into the
channel that we had previously made carried us more than
a ship's length farther this time. Again we floundered
deep in the sand, and again the ribs creaked as if they
would break. But with groaning effort, the powerful
machine brought us back to the buoy again.

Now the pilot sounded the course that we had dredged
and came up with the heartening cry, "It can be done! Now
stoke the fires well and steer carefully!" But the cargo
was shifted before we proceeded, and the cotton was moved
to one side of the ship, so that it lay on its side and raised
its keel. The run began. The wheels splashed water around
wildly, and the vessel was flying along. Then the keel
scraped bottom. The ship ran aground three times, and
then it rumbled up to the pilot light, sliding gently on the

sand, and floated off in the ocean, buoyant as a swan. Our hearts beat loud. But not all obstacles had been overcome, for before us the fox lurked for his prey, and a raging storm began to whip its waves straight into our faces. The method by which the narrow channels in the sandbanks were passed was highly ingenious. Lights on the islands, unseen by the enemy, gave us alignments to those points where the pilot had to order a change of course. Our white lantern on the stern was exchanged for a red one when we ran aground, and the friendly light immediately gave us a signal as to how we could get afloat. The lights finally came to an end, and the sea and the fleet lay before us.

"Dark night, cover us with thy protecting mantle and conceal us from all eyes! But a Supreme Being keeps watch above and will not let us perish without plan or purpose!" The moon has sunk below the horizon an hour before this time, but its gentle light is still hovering over the heavens, which gratefully reflect its glow! The ship is as silent as a tomb, and all eyes are prying through the darkness, anxiously searching. "Look there! Is that a cloud? A shadow? A ship? It resolves itself into vague, nebulous forms on the horizon, for the storm is roaring madly. Thank heavens, we are safe!"

We moved over the billowing sea like a pale shadow. The passengers were amazed at the indigo blue waters of the Gulf Stream and at the raging of the elements, and they were surprised at the speed of the voyage and the shining of the sea at night. But soon the specter of seasickness lay over the ship, bringing down everyone from commander to passengers. We would lie in the fresh air between the bales of cotton and read very good books from the ship's library. I used the trip as a cure, fasted for three days (less one hour), and then carefully accustomed myself again to food, and my still exhausted body felt regenerated. But again it seemed as if the journey would end disastrously. The worried commander sat with the captain and reckoned, for the Bermudas are a very small group of islands in the wide ocean and are hard to find when the sun, the point of reference for the reckonings, can not be seen. The engineer would stick his head in the cabin from time to time and would mutter unintelligible numbers. "What is it?" "The coal is about gone!" The mast was already being examined to see how many cords of firewood it would yield, together with the deck. We would not be able to reach the island if the adverse wind continued or if we steered a false course, and we would be forced to abandon ship at sea and seek safety in boats on the open ocean, with the single hope of being discovered by enemy ships. But the wind subsided, the sun broke cheerfully through the clouds, and the chronometers and tables were quickly brought out. "Land must appear on the starboard side!" the commander called out gleefully. He was right. Soon "Bermuda, the Queen," greeted us in the calm, emerald-green water.

It is really a rare pleasure to wander around on the islands, among the tropical plants and the white houses, in the dark avenues of cypresses, or along the seashore, the washed, jagged, coral rocks of which form the strangest structures, against which the ocean hurls its white foam, fashioning new shapes and new burlesque figures. The sea is as green on the horizon, as azure blue and transparent as the purest crystal glass. Observed from the heights, the thousand little islands seem to rise from the sea, adorned with neat little white houses that enliven the picture everywhere. Indeed, the roofs are also white and clean as snow to catch every drop of rain water, which is the only drink here, since no spring flows from the porous, rocky islands.

The green, undulating island hills which crown the steep, gray rocks, the azure mirror in which the Queen sees her image, the white villas and forts that lie like enamel in emerald-green adornment—these are not the only things that make my heart glad, but so does the glorious feeling: You are on the way home. Behind me lie the dangers wrought by human hands. Behind me lie battle, war, destruction, hatred, and devastation! Before me—peace and my homeland!

We received no news of the three steamers that left

Wilmington with us. Did the storm destroy them? Or the
Yankees capture them? Or were they swallowed up by the
waves? We could be fervently grateful to God!

One day the officers of the English Corps of Engineers
and of the Artillery invited me to mess. I borrowed the
inevitable frock coat and top hat from James, the painter,
who was very devoted to me, and who worked magic with
seascapes, and I spent a cheerful evening sitting between
the two colonels.

The baths are splendid! "The sun is rising from its light
bed of azure! Come, shake off your laziness! We will bathe
in waves such as wash Mother Earth nowhere else!" "Too
early?" "Too cold?" "Well then, with you alone, dear
Major Meredith! Let the others stretch their sleepy limbs!"
Passing through jagged, rocky crevices, the cool sea surges
around our limbs. "It is cold; but quickly, with two jumps,
into the clear flood, along which the sun draws its golden
stripes. Delightful waves!"

> We shout and rejoice in the waves with keen delight,
> And with throbbing hearts we bathe in the high, splash-
> ing foam!

We swim from rock to rock across the water, the bottom
of which can be seen at a depth of forty feet. Snow-white
sand welcomes our feet on the shore, and shells can be had
for the seeking. Crabs are in the rocky cavities, and the
sea washes up coral growth and strange formations on the
lonely island. Everything is amusing! All is strange!

We came out of the water with new vigor and fresh life,
and with double delight we greeted the sun, the landscape,
and the blue sea. With doubled animation we looked forward to breakfast, the sweet aroma of which was wafted
toward us as from the grill. A loud cheer for the Bermuda
Sea!

On a splendid morning we seated ourselves in a buggy, an
American coach that is as light as a feather, and we drove
merrily and cheerfully along the harbor of St. George's (for
that was the name of the town that we were in), with the

greenish-blue sea always at our side. We crossed on the ferry at the lonely Martell's Tower and drove southward around Harrison Sound between splendid groups of rocks, beneath which the sea often lay concealed in "purplish-blue," and on through fragrant, pretty forests of oleanders, in which blue and red birds drew our attention. A small species of dove that also nests in the wild here greeted us with coos. We reached Flatsville, on a picturesque bay, and after a truly poetic trip we finally rode into the City of Hamilton, where we met our friendly passengers of the *A. D. Vance*. Leading them was Colonel Crossan, who received us with champagne, and to whom I had to present, for his wife, a painting of his ship breaking through the blockade.

But everything must come to an end. The steamer *Alpha* (Captain Hunter) brought us from the magic island to Halifax in fine weather on October 4. On the way I caught broken bone fever, which was epidemic in Bermuda, and which weakened me very much. But thanks to the careful attention of my fellow passengers, among them Captain Turner, C. S. A., I had recovered three days after my arrival to the extent that I made the old English hotel resound with merry German tunes.

Halifax Harbor rivals the harbor of Bermuda in beauty, but its water lacks the ethereal color, which is supposed to have caused Shakespeare to set his *Tempest* play there. Indeed, the Bermuda Islands fill an entire body of literature, since almost all important English authors have chosen them as subjects to celebrate in song.

The City of Halifax, constructed almost entirely of wood, is large and extensive. Only four or five sections have quite new, massive homes, which are distinguished by splendid sculpture.

Facing the harbor lies Drotham [*sic*] with the famous railroad that even transports ships from the harbor to the high level of the canals connecting the lakes of Nova Scotia. Here by the lakes I found genuine northern nature in its most beautiful fall dress (October 6). There were northern conifers, and among them succulent, wavy moss, and grass, and rocks that jut forth in reddish color. Springs bubble up everywhere, and moist dew makes the colors vivid. The air is fresh, full, and clear, its fragrance filling the chest, and it is a pleasure to wander along the lakes garlanded with woods and lying high above the sea.

Dirty Indian children in shirts jump out of four or five wigwams standing on the southeast side of a hill and beg, "A cent, a cent!" They are full of fire, cheerful, and in high spirits, despite the fact that they are covered with dirt. The wigwams are made of birch poles with rough bark fastened around them.

The dull, braided hair that hangs shaggily around the yellowish-brown faces of the Indians is characteristic. These people's hunger for freedom, apart from their bad qualities, is impressive, and their love of independence is great. The Indian is a born nobleman. In the midst of the great culture that surrounds him, he goes around proud as a lion in his dirty jewels and costumes, which are still important to him, and he scorns the world that bows down before mammon and bends its neck under the yoke of a thousand needs. He wants to be free of the tyranny of the "pale faces" and the despotism of the moneybag.

On the steamer *Europa*, commanded by the likable old Captain Shannon, we said farewell to land and were carried eastward in good weather and on a beautiful sea, together with a multitude of passengers, mostly Yankee families. To be mentioned among the companions on the voyage is Pierre d'Orleans, Prince of Joinville, grandson of Louis Phillip, an inoffensive, pleasant young man who played shuffleboard most enthusiastically with us. Major Anderson of the British Embassy in Washington gave me as an eyewitness some interesting information about the doings of the Northern Government and did much to strengthen me in my political opinions. He was a calm, intelligent gentleman who looked upon the world with complete objectivity.[3]

---

[3] Lonn, p. 364, emphasizes Scheibert's condescending attitude toward the French prince. It will be recalled that, while Scheibert served the

We welcomed with jubilation the first strand of Europe, Ireland's blissful coast. Again we greeted Queenstown and the Irish Sea in favorable light, and at last we landed in Liverpool, where I received my first comforting letters from home, which I opened with true anxiety and excitement to see whether everyone was present and in good health. Thank heavens, all was as I had wished at heart, but as I had hardly dared hope it would be. I could have shouted my happiness to the streets, and I laughed to myself so much throughout the evening that I even attracted the attention of passers-by. It was more, indeed, much more than I deserved. All things are given unto us here on earth! All through grace! *Nothing* is merited!

END

Bibliography

Books and Articles

Allgemeine Deutsche Biographie. Leipsig, 1907. 56 vols.

Blackford, William W. *War Years With Jeb Stuart.* New York, 1945.

Borcke, Heros von. *Memoirs of the Confederate War for Independence.* London and Edinburgh, 1866. 2 vols.

————. *Zwei Yahre im Sattel und am Feinde; errinnerungen aus dem unabhängigkeitskriege der Konföderirten . . . .* Berlin, 1898. 2 vols.

Bradford, Gamaliel. *Confederate Portraits.* New York, 1914.

Chesney, C. C. *Campaigns in Virginia, Maryland, etc. . . .* London, 1865. 2 vols.

[Cooke, John Esten]. *Life of Stonewall Jackson . . . .* New York, 1863.

Coulter, E. M. *Travels in the Confederate States . . . .* Norman, 1948.

Dabney, R. L. *Life and Campaigns of Lieut.-Gen. Thomas J. Jackson.* New York and Richmond, 1866.

DeLeon, T. C. *Belles, Beauxs and Brains of the 60's.* New York, 1907.

Freeman, Douglas Southall. *R. E. Lee: A Biography.* New York, 1935. 4 vols.

Fremantle, Arthur J. L. *Three Months in the Southern States, April-June, 1863.* Mobile, 1864.

Girard, Charles Frédéric. *Les États Confédérés d' Amerique Visités en 1863.* Paris, 1864.

Hardee, William J. *Rifle and Infantry Tactics* . . . . Mobile, 1861, 1863.

Harrison, Mrs. Burton. *Recollections Grave and Gay*. New York, 1911.

[Hood, Gen. John B.]. "Letter from General John B. Hood," *Southern Historical Society Papers*, IV, 145-150 (Oct., 1877).

Hoole, Wm. Stanley. "Alabama-Built Submarine Was First to Sink a Battleship," *Birmingham News Monthy Magazine*, Dec. 13, 1953, pp. 12-13.

————. *Vizetelly Covers the Confederacy* (Confederate Centennial Studies, No. 4). Tuscaloosa, 1957.

Hume, Edgar E. "Colonel Heros von Borcke. A Famous Prussian Volunteer in the Confederate States Army," *Southern Sketches*, 1 Series, No. 2. Charlottesville, 1935.

Johnson, John. *Defense of Charleston Harbor* . . . *1863-1865*. Charleston, 1890.

Jones, J. Wm. *Christ in the Camp, or Religion in Lee's Army*. Richmond, 1887.

Kaufmann, Wilhelm. *Die Deutschen im amerikanischen Bürgerkriege (Sezessionskrieg 1861-1865)*. München und Berlin, 1911.

Kelln, Albert. "Confederate Submarines," *Virginia Magazine of History and Biography*, LXI, 293-303 (July, 1953).

Langer, W. L., ed. *Encyclopedia of World History*. Boston, 1948.

Lawley, Francis. Essays in London *Times*, Oct. 7, 1862-Apr. 29, 1865.

Lonn, Ella. *Foreigners in the Confederacy*. Chapel Hill, 1940.

Luvaas, Jay. "A Prussian Observer with Lee," *Military Affairs*, XXI, 105-117 (Fall, 1957).

————, ed. G. F. R. Henderson, *The Civil War: A Soldier's View*. Chicago, 1958.

Miller, Francis T., ed. *Photographic History of the Civil War*. New York, 1911. 10 vols.

Nichols, James L. *Confederate Engineers* (Confederate Centennial Studies, No. 5). Tuscaloosa, 1957.

Official Records of the Union and Confederate Navies of the War of the Rebellion. Washington, 1894-1927. 31 vols.

Poindexter, Charles "Major J. Scheibert (of the Prussian Army) on Confederate History," *SHSP*, XVIII, 422-428 (Dec., 1890).

Richardson, James D., ed. *Compilation of the Messages and Papers of the Confederacy* . . . . Nashville, 1906. 2 vols.

Roman, Alfred. *Military Operations of General Beauregard* . . . . New York, 1884. 2 vols.

Rosengarten, J. G. *German Soldiers in the Wars of the United States*. Philadelphia, 1886.

Ross, Fitzgerald. *A Visit to the Cities and Camps of the Confederate States*. London, 1865.

Taylor, Thomas E. *Running the Blockade* . . . . New York, 1896.

Venable, C. S. "Major Scheibert's Book," *SHSP*, IV, 88-91 (Aug., 1877).

Vizetelly, Frank. "Charleston Under Fire," *Cornhill Magazine*, X, 90-110 (July, 1864).

Von Achten der Letzte. Amerikanische Kriegsbilder aus der Südarmee des Generals Robert E. Lee. Wiesbaden, 1871.

War of the Rebellion: A Compilation of the Official Records of the Union and Confederate Armies. Washington, 1880-1901. 128 vols.

Letters

Gen. R. E. Lee to Col. Stapleton Crutchfield, Headquarters, Army of Northern Virginia, Feb. 15, 1864.

To Wm. Stanley Hoole: Stanislaw Badony, Miejska Biblioteka Publiczna, Szczecin, Poland, Apr. 3, 1957; Edward A. Symans, American Embassy, Warsaw, Poland, Apr. 12, 1957; Jay Luvaas, Allegheny College, Pa., March 3, 1958; Alexander C. Niven, Washington University, St. Louis, Mo., Nov. 18, 22, 26, Dec. 2, 6, 11, 20, 1957; Feb. 6, May 4, 1958. (All letters are in the University of Alabama Library, University, Ala.)

Justus Scheibert's Writings—A Selection

"Befestigungs-Ideen. Eine erwiderung auf die 'Ideen über Befestigungen' von K. H.," *Jahrbücher für die deutsche Armee und Marine,* LXVII (Juni, 1888).

Die Befestigungskunst und die Lehre von Kampfe. Berlin, 1880-1883. 3 vols.

"Beiträge zur charakterschilderung des Reiter-Generals J. E. B. Stuart," *Jahrbücher* . . . , LXIX (Sept., 1888).

Der Bürgerkrieg in den nordamerikanischen Staaten. Militairisch beleuchtet für den deutschen Offizier. Berlin, 1874.

Einfluss der neuesten Taktik und der gezogenen Waffen auf den Festungskrieg . . . . Berlin, 1861.

The Franco-German War 1870-1871. Tr. . . . by Major J. A. Ferrier and Mrs. Ferrier. Chatham, 1894.

"Das Gefecht im Beginn des Sezessionskriege," *Jahrbücher* . . . , LXXXIV (Aug., 1892).

"General J. E. B. Stuart," *ibid.,* XXV (Dez., 1877).

"General J. E. B. Stuart's letzter grofser Raid," *ibid.,* XXXIII (Nov., Dez., 1879).

"General Robert E. Lee, Oberkommandeur der ehemaligen südstaatlichen Armee in Nord-Amerika, *ibid.,* XVI (Sept., 1875).

La Guerre Civile aux États-Unis d' Amerique (Guerre de la Sécession) .... Tr. par J. Bornecque .... Paris, 1876.

La Guerre Franco-Allemande de 1870-1871 .... tr. sur la 2. éd. allemande par Ernest Jaeglé .... Paris, 1891.

Illustrirtes deutsches Militär-Lexikon .... Berlin, 1877.

"Jefferson Davis, Präsident der einstigen cönfederierten Staaten (auch ein Soldatenleben)," *Jahrbücher* ... , LXXXI (Dez., 1891).

"Jefferson Davis, President of the Late Confederate States," *SHSP*, XIX, 406-416 (Dec., 1891).

Der Krieg zwischen Frankreich und Deutschland in den Jähren 1870-71. Berlin, 1891.

"Letter from Major Scheibert," *SHSP*, IX, 570-572 (Dec., 1881).

"Letter from Maj. Scheibert, of the Prussian Royal Engineers," *ibid.*, V, 90-93 (Jan.-Feb., 1877).

"Die letzten Tage der Rebellion. Aus dem Tagebuche eines Kannoniers," *Jahrbücher* ... , LI (April, 1884).

"Major Scheibert (of the Prussian Army) on Confederate History," *SHSP*, XVIII, 423-428 (Dec., 1890).

Mit Schwert und Feder. Erinnerungen aus meinem Leben. Berlin, 1902.

"Neuere Schriften über Landesverteidig und Befestigungswesen," *Jahrbücher* ... , LXIV (Aug., 1887).

"Oberst J. S. Mosby," *ibid.*, XVIII (Jan., 1876).

"Reiterskizzen aus dem amerkanische Bürgerkriege," *ibid.*, LXXV (April, Juni, 1890).

"Shermans Marsch durch Georgien. Ein Beitrag zur Geschichte des Sezessionskrieges," *ibid.*, LVIII (Jan., Febr., Marz., 1886).

Sieben Monate in den Rebellion-Staaten während des nordamerikanischen Krieges 1863. Stettin, 1868.

"Stonewall Jackson," *Jahrbücher* . . . , XVII, (Okt., Nov., 1875).

"Stonewall Jacksons Virginienthal-Campagne," *ibid.*, XXXI (Mai, Juni, 1879).

"Uber das Festungswesen," *ibid.*, LXII (Marz, 1887).

"Der verhängrifsvolle Minenkrater bei Petersburg. Eine Episode aus dem Sezessionskriege," *ibid.*, XCII (Aug., 1894).

Das Zusammenwirken der Armee und Marine. Eine Studie illustrirt durch den Kampf um den Mississippi, 1861-63 . . . . Rathenow, [1887].

———— and Heros von Borcke. *Der grosse Reiterschlacht bei Brandy Station, 9, juni, 1863* . . . . Berlin, 1893.

———— and W. Porth. *Illustrirtes Militär-Lexikon fur die K. und K. österreichischungarische und deutsche Armee* . . . . Berlin, 1897.

Scheibert Index, by Robert K. Krick

All geographical locations are in Virginia unless otherwise specified.